RAISING RESILIENT HEARTS

GUIDED STRATEGIES TO MASTER THE ART OF EFFICIENT PARENTING

Simplify Your Approach,
Amplify Your Impact

NIRAIMATHI MAGILMARAN

INDIA · SINGAPORE · MALAYSIA

ISBN 979-8-89415-380-3

"In the Chaos find the Beauty of Parenthood's Rhythm"

Contents

A Note from the Author

Welcome to the pages of our shared journey, where the art of parenting collides with the challenges of our modern age. As we stand at the crossroads of screens and societal expectations, the path to efficient parenting seems shrouded in a haze of contradictory advice and overwhelming choices. Yet, fear not, for in this conversation, we will unravel the complexities together, much like old friends sipping coffee, sharing stories, and exchanging wisdom.

Have you ever found yourself pondering the intricacies of guiding your child through the maze of technology, where screens dictate a significant part of their reality? Or perhaps you've wrestled with the delicate balance of nurturing their independence while instilling the values that echo through generations? These are the questions that echo in the hearts of parents, and it is precisely these questions that propel us into the heart of efficient parenting.

In this journey, my role is not that of an all-knowing sage but rather a companion, a fellow traveller navigating the challenges of parenthood. Drawing inspiration from mentors who have walked this path before me, I invite you to join a dialogue that goes beyond theories and prescriptions.

As we navigate the nuances of modern parenting, my perspective is grounded in a pragmatic ethos – one that acknowledges the realities of your daily life. It's about taking the abstract and distilling it into tangible, actionable steps that you can seamlessly integrate into your family's rhythm. Every piece of advice isn't a lofty ideal but a practical strategy, a tool in your hands to transform challenges into opportunities for growth.

Throughout our exploration, I'll share not only the findings of research and the perspectives of experts but also the lived experiences of real families. It's about injecting authenticity into our conversation, making the journey relatable and, above all, empowering. Because, dear reader, this is not just a book; it's a toolkit for your parenting endeavour. It's an invitation to ponder, reflect, and, most importantly, act.

So, with a cup of coffee in hand and an open heart, let's embark on this journey together. Let's delve into the depths of modern parenting, armed with insights that blend inspiration with practicality. The challenges are real, but so is our capacity to overcome them. Welcome to a transformative exploration of efficient parenting, where every page holds not just words but the keys to unlocking a happier, more harmonious family life.

Introduction

Unveiling the Essence of Efficient Parenting Strategies

Why Efficient Parenting?

Efficient parenting is like finding the perfect balance between being a nurturing guide and setting boundaries that help children thrive. It's not about being a superhero parent but rather about making intentional choices that promote a healthy family dynamic. When parents are efficient, they create an environment where communication flows, responsibilities are shared, and each family member feels valued. This approach fosters emotional well-being, resilience, and a sense of security in children. In essence, efficient parenting sets the stage for a harmonious family life, where everyone can grow and flourish.

In the realm of efficient parenting, adaptability is key. Recognizing and responding to the unique needs of each child, understanding that there's no one-size-fits-all approach, contributes to a positive family atmosphere. It involves active listening, providing support without overbearing control, and encouraging open dialogue. As parents efficiently navigate the challenges and triumphs of child-rearing, they model valuable life skills for their children. This not only enhances family well-being but also equips youngsters with the tools they need to face the world outside their home. The ripple effect of efficient parenting extends beyond the family unit, shaping future generations and fostering a more compassionate society.

The Fundamental Need: Nurturing a Strong Foundation:

Efficient parenting begins with the recognition that we are not merely raising children; we are shaping the architects of our future society. The need for a strong foundation is paramount. It's about laying the groundwork for resilience, emotional well-being, and a sense of responsibility – qualities that will serve our children in a world that is both interconnected and ever-changing. But how do we go about building such a foundation? It starts with intentionality – a deliberate, thoughtful approach to parenting that prioritizes long-term outcomes over short-term fixes. We must ask ourselves: What values do we want to instill in our children? What lessons do we want them to carry with them into adulthood?

From there, it's about creating an environment that fosters growth and development. This means providing opportunities for exploration and discovery, allowing our children to learn through both success and failure. It means cultivating open lines of communication, where thoughts and feelings are met with understanding and empathy. It also involves setting boundaries and expectations, teaching our children the importance of accountability and self-discipline. It's about striking a delicate balance between nurturing support and empowering independence, guiding our children as they navigate the complexities of the world around them.

Ultimately, nurturing a strong foundation is about planting seeds of possibility – seeds that will germinate and flourish over time, shaping the trajectory of our children's lives. It's a journey that requires patience, perseverance, and a steadfast commitment to our children's growth and well-being. Let us remember the profound impact we have as parents. Let us embrace the responsibility of shaping the next generation with humility and grace. And let us hold fast to the belief that, with the right foundation in place, our children will be equipped to thrive in whatever challenges lie ahead.

Balancing Act: Navigating the Modern Landscape:

In the labyrinth of modern parenting, the terrain we traverse is fraught with complexities as diverse as they are daunting. The digital age has ushered in a new era, where screens and social media loom large, presenting both opportunities and challenges in equal measure. At the heart of efficient parenting lays a delicate balancing act—a dance between harnessing the benefits of technology while safeguarding against its potential pitfalls. In efficient parenting demands, we equip ourselves with the tools to navigate this digital terrain with grace and discernment. It's about striking a balance between embracing technology as a tool for learning and exploration, while also setting boundaries to protect our children from its more harmful effects. It's about fostering a healthy relationship with screens, where devices are seen as tools for connection rather than distractions from it.

But finding this balance is no easy feat. It requires constant vigilance, a willingness to adapt, and a keen understanding of the unique needs and challenges our families are facing. It's about cultivating mindfulness in our digital consumption, modelling healthy habits for our children, and creating spaces within our homes where technology takes a backseat to human connection. Efficient parenting is not about demonizing technology or retreating from the digital world altogether. Instead, it's about harnessing its power in service of our family's values and priorities. It's about using technology as a tool to enrich our lives, rather than allowing it to dictate our behaviour or erode the fabric of our relationships.

As we navigate this ever-evolving landscape together, let us approach the challenges of modern parenting with curiosity, resilience, and a commitment to finding balance amidst the chaos. Let us embrace the opportunities that technology affords us, while also remaining vigilant in protecting what matters most—our connection to one another. In doing so, we can cultivate a family life that is both connected and nurturing, thriving in the digital age without losing sight of what truly matters.

Crafting Individualized Strategies:

In the intricate medley of family life, one truth reigns supreme: no two families are alike. Each household is a unique ecosystem, shaped by its own dynamics, values, and personalities. Recognizing this fundamental diversity is at the core of efficient parenting—a philosophy that celebrates the individuality of each child and family unit.

Efficient parenting isn't about adhering to a rigid set of rules or following a one-size-fits-all approach. Instead, it's about crafting individualized strategies that are tailored to the specific needs and dynamics of your family. This personalized approach ensures that the strategies you employ resonate with your values, preferences, and circumstances, fostering an environment where both parents and children can thrive.

As we embark on this journey together, it's important to remember that efficient parenting is not about striving for perfection. It's about making progress, one step at a time, as we navigate the ever-changing landscape of family life. It's a mindful exploration, a continuous dialogue between generations, and an invitation to cultivate a resilient and harmonious family dynamic.

So, let's dive into the heart of efficient parenting strategies, where every action becomes a brushstroke, contributing to the masterpiece of "Raising Resilient Hearts." Let's welcome it with open arms, the uniqueness of our families, celebrate the diversity of our experiences, and commit ourselves to creating a nurturing environment where our children can thrive and flourish. Together, let's get going on this journey of growth, learning, and love, as we craft personalized strategies that honour the individuality of our families and pave the way for a brighter future.

"At the end of the day, the most Overwhelming key to a child's success is the positive involvement of **Parents**"

Chapter 1

Navigating Modern Parenting Challenges

1.1 Digital Dilemma: The Screen Time Struggle

In the age of ubiquitous screens, parents face the challenge of managing their children's screen usage into a valuable tool for learning and connection rather than a source of isolation. Tech Tensions emerge as a significant challenge. Beyond the mere screen time conundrum, parents grapple with the complexities of technology, encompassing issues such as online safety, cyber bullying, and digital etiquette. In the case of efficient parenting the task goes beyond setting arbitrary limits; it's about transforming digital age demands, not only the limitation of device usage but also the proactive education of children to navigate the intricate digital maze responsibly. This digital dilemma requires a nuanced approach rooted in practical strategies, fostering a balance that enhances family life.

Understanding the Issue:

The first step in addressing the screen time struggle is recognizing its multifaceted nature. The surge in screen time among children, driven by the ubiquity of digital devices, has raised concerns about its impact on their physical and mental well-being. The ramifications extend beyond the screen itself, affecting crucial aspects of their development and family relationships.

Online Safety concerns:

In the vast expanse of the digital world, the concept of online safety looms large, casting a shadow over the seemingly boundless opportunities for connectivity and exploration. With every click, tap, and swipe, parents are faced with the daunting task of safeguarding their children from a myriad of potential threats and dangers that lurk within the virtual landscape.

At the forefront of these concerns lies the spectre of exposure to inappropriate content—a pervasive issue that has only been exacerbated by the omnipresence of the internet. From explicit images and videos to violent or extremist ideologies, the digital realm is rife with content that is wholly unsuitable for young eyes. As parents, it falls upon us to erect digital barriers and establish age-appropriate boundaries to shield our children from harm's way.

Yet, the dangers of the online world extend far beyond mere exposure to inappropriate content. In recent years, the rise of online predators has emerged as a chilling reality, preying upon unsuspecting children through social media platforms, online gaming communities, and other digital avenues. These predators employ sophisticated tactics to manipulate and exploit their young victims, posing a grave threat to their safety and well-being.

Furthermore, the inadvertent sharing of personal information represents yet another perilous pitfall in the digital age. Whether it's a seemingly innocent post on social media or an ill-advised click on a phishing email, the consequences of oversharing can be far-reaching and profound. From identity theft and cyber bullying to online harassment and stalking, the risks associated with the dissemination of personal information are manifold and alarming.

Navigating these virtual minefields requires a combination of vigilance, education, and proactive engagement on the part of parents. It's about fostering open lines of communication with our children, equipping them with the knowledge and skills to recognize and respond to online threats, and establishing clear guidelines for safe and responsible digital behaviour.

But perhaps most importantly, it's about cultivating a culture of trust and support within our families—a safe haven where our children feel comfortable coming to us with their concerns and seeking guidance in times of need. In the digital age, the task of ensuring our children's online safety may seem daunting, but with diligence, determination, and a commitment to their well-being, we can navigate these virtual landscapes and empower our children to thrive in the digital world while keeping them safe from harm.

Cyber bullying Risks:

In the digital age, the risk of cyber bullying looms large, casting a shadow over the interconnected world in which our children navigate. With the prevalence of technology and the omnipresence of social media platforms, the risk of cyber bullying has become an ever-present reality, posing significant threats to our children's emotional well-being and mental health.

Cyber bullying takes many forms, from hurtful comments and derogatory messages to the malicious spreading of rumours and the creation of fake profiles for the purpose of harassment. These harmful interactions often occur in the seemingly anonymous realm of online spaces, where the perpetrators feel emboldened to unleash their cruelty from behind the safety of a screen.

Efficient parenting in the digital age requires a multifaceted approach to addressing the risks of cyber bullying. It begins with education and awareness, equipping both parents and children with the knowledge and skills to recognize the signs of cyber bullying and respond appropriately. This involves teaching our children the importance of digital etiquette and responsibility—instilling in them a sense of empathy, kindness, and respect for others in their online interactions.

But detection is only half the battle. Efficient parenting also entails creating a supportive environment where our children feel comfortable confiding in us about their experiences with cyber bullying. This requires open communication, active listening, and a non-judgmental approach to discussing sensitive topics. By fostering a culture of trust and transparency within our families, we can empower our children to seek help and support when they encounter cyber bullying, rather than suffering in silence.

Furthermore, efficient parenting involves proactive engagement with our children's digital lives, monitoring their online activities, and setting clear boundaries and expectations for their behaviour online. This includes teaching them how to protect their privacy, safeguard their personal information, and block or report abusive users or content.

Ultimately, efficient parenting in the digital age is about arming our children with the knowledge, skills, and support they need to navigate the online world safely and responsibly. It's about fostering resilience in the face of adversity, cultivating empathy and kindness in their interactions with others, and creating a supportive family environment where they feel valued, heard, and empowered to thrive in both the digital realm and the real world.

Digital Etiquette and Responsibility:

In the ever-evolving landscape of the digital age, the concept of digital etiquette and responsibility has emerged as a critical aspect of parenting. As technology continues to reshape the way we communicate, connect, and conduct ourselves in the online world, parents are faced with the formidable task of instilling in their children a sense of responsibility and mindfulness regarding their digital behaviour.

Digital etiquette encompasses a wide range of principles and practices governing how individuals interact and communicate in digital spaces. From basic manners such as using polite language and refraining from cyber bullying to more complex considerations such as respecting others' privacy and intellectual property, digital etiquette plays a vital role in fostering a positive and respectful online environment.

Efficient parenting requires a proactive approach to teaching children about digital etiquette and responsibility from a young age. This involves setting clear expectations and boundaries for their online behaviour, emphasizing the importance of treating others with kindness and respect, and teaching them how to navigate the complexities of digital communication with integrity and empathy.

Moreover, parents must educate their children about the consequences of their digital actions and the long-term impact of their digital footprint. In an age where every post, comment, and interaction leaves a permanent trace online, it's essential for children to understand the significance of their online presence and the potential repercussions of their online behaviour on their future relationships, education, and career prospects.

Efficient parenting also entails leading by example, modelling positive digital behaviour and practicing good digital citizenship ourselves. By demonstrating empathy, integrity, and responsibility in our own online interactions, we can instill these values in our children and empower them to become responsible digital citizens.

Ultimately, digital etiquette and responsibility are not just about following a set of rules; they're about cultivating a mindset of respect, empathy, and accountability in our children's digital lives. By equipping them with the knowledge, skills, and values they need to navigate the digital world with integrity and confidence, we can help them harness the power of technology for positive change and contribute to a more inclusive, respectful, and compassionate online community.

Physical Health Implications:

The prevalence of screens in our daily lives has ushered in a new era of convenience, connectivity, and unprecedented access to information. However, alongside these benefits, excessive screen time has emerged as a significant concern for children's physical health. Research has revealed a myriad of implications associated with prolonged screen exposure, ranging from sedentary behaviours to a host of physical health issues that can impact children's overall well-being.

One of the primary concerns associated with excessive screen time is its link to sedentary behaviours. With the allure of digital entertainment and the convenience of handheld devices, children are spending more time than ever sitting in front of screens, often at the expense of physical activity. This sedentary lifestyle has been implicated in a range of health problems, including obesity, cardiovascular disease, and metabolic disorders.

Indeed, numerous studies have demonstrated a clear correlation between increased screen time and a higher likelihood of obesity among children and adolescents. The sedentary nature of screen-based activities, coupled with exposure to food advertisements and the tendency to snack while watching screens, can contribute to unhealthy eating habits and weight gain over time.

In addition to obesity, excessive screen time has also been linked to disrupted sleep patterns, another critical aspect of children's physical health. The blue light emitted by screens can interfere with the body's natural sleep-wake cycle, making it difficult for children to fall asleep and stay asleep. This can lead to sleep deprivation, which has been associated with a host of negative health outcomes, including impaired cognitive function, mood disturbances, and increased risk of chronic diseases.

Furthermore, prolonged screen time can also contribute to musculoskeletal problems, particularly among children who spend long hours hunched over electronic devices. Poor posture and repetitive movements associated with screen use can lead to a range of issues, including neck and back pain, eye strain, and carpal tunnel syndrome. These physical discomforts can have a significant impact on children's quality of life, affecting their ability to concentrate, participate in physical activities, and engage in everyday tasks.

Moreover, prolonged periods of inactivity associated with excessive screen time can hinder the development of essential motor skills and physical fitness in children. Physical activity is crucial for promoting healthy growth and development, strengthening muscles and bones, and improving cardiovascular health. However, when children spend extended periods in front of screens, they miss out on opportunities to engage in active play and exercise, which are essential for building strength, coordination, and endurance.

As parents, it's essential to be mindful of the amount of time our children spend in front of screens and to prioritize activities that promote physical activity, healthy sleep habits, and overall wellness. By striking a balance between screen time and other activities, we can help our children lead healthier, happier lives now and in the future.

Mental Health Challenges:

The intersection of technology and mental health has emerged as a pressing concern, particularly when it comes to children and adolescents. Prolonged screen exposure has been linked to a host of mental health challenges, ranging from heightened levels of stress and anxiety to an increased risk of depression. The constant influx of information, coupled with virtual interactions and digital distractions, can overwhelm young minds, impacting their emotional well-being and resilience in profound ways.

One of the primary mental health challenges associated with excessive screen time is the heightened levels of stress and anxiety experienced by children. The relentless stream of notifications, updates, and messages can create a sense of constant connectivity and pressure to stay plugged in at all times. This constant state of hyper arousal can elevate stress levels, leading to feelings of overwhelm, agitation, and emotional exhaustion.

Moreover, the virtual world presents a unique set of challenges for children when it comes to managing anxiety. Social media platforms, in particular, can serve as breeding grounds for comparison, judgment, and peer pressure, exacerbating feelings of inadequacy and self-doubt. The curated nature of online personas and the pressure to present a perfect image can contribute to a distorted sense of reality, leading children to feel isolated and disconnected from their peers.

In addition to stress and anxiety, prolonged screen exposure has also been linked to an increased risk of depression among children and adolescents. Research suggests that excessive screen time can disrupt sleep patterns, interfere with social interactions, and exacerbate feelings of loneliness and isolation—all of which are risk factors for depression. Moreover, the constant barrage of negative news, cyber bullying, and online harassment can further erode children's mental well-being, leaving them feeling helpless and hopeless in the face of adversity.

Furthermore, the digital world can impact children's emotional regulation and resilience, essential skills for navigating life's challenges. The instant gratification culture perpetuated by screens can undermine children's ability to cope with stress and frustration, leading to difficulties in regulating their emotions and managing conflict effectively. Moreover, the constant exposure to virtual interactions can desensitize children to real-world emotions and social cues, making it harder for them to form meaningful connections and empathize with others.

The digital dilemma extends beyond physical health concerns to encompass mental well-being as well. Prolonged screen exposure has been associated with heightened levels of stress, anxiety, and depression in children, as well as challenges in emotional regulation and resilience. As parents, it's essential to be mindful of the impact of screens on our children's mental health and to prioritize activities that promote emotional well-being, such as spending time outdoors, engaging in creative pursuits, and fostering meaningful connections with others. By striking a balance between screen time and other activities, we can help our children develop the skills and resilience they need to thrive in an increasingly digital world.

Isolation from Family Bonding:

One of the gravest concerns surrounding excessive screen time is the potential isolation from family bonding it can induce. As children become increasingly engrossed in screens—whether it be smartphones, tablets, computers, or gaming consoles—they may withdraw from face-to-face interactions with family members, peers, and other caregivers. This withdrawal not only hinders the development of crucial social skills but also weakens the fabric of the family unit, eroding the quality of relationships and diminishing opportunities for meaningful connection.

Family bonding, a cornerstone of family life, becomes compromised in the face of excessive screen time. Instead of engaging in shared activities, conversations, and experiences, family members may find themselves physically present but emotionally absent, each immersed in their own digital worlds. The intimate moments of connection that were once cherished—such as family dinners, game nights, or outings—

may be overshadowed by the allure of screens, leaving little room for genuine interaction and engagement.

The isolation induced by extensive screen time can have profound implications for children's social development and emotional well-being. Human connection is essential for nurturing empathy, building interpersonal skills, and fostering a sense of belonging and security. When children spend excessive amounts of time in front of screens, they miss out on valuable opportunities to practice these skills in real-world interactions, leading to difficulties in forming meaningful relationships and navigating social situations effectively.

The withdrawal from family bonding that accompanies excessive screen time can contribute to feelings of disconnection and alienation within the family unit. Instead of fostering a sense of togetherness and unity, screens can create barriers between family members, hindering communication, understanding, and intimacy. Family members may struggle to connect on a deeper level, leading to feelings of loneliness, frustration, and resentment.

Efficient parenting requires a proactive approach to addressing the isolation from family bonding that extensive screen time can induce. It involves setting clear boundaries and expectations around screen use, establishing designated screen-free times and spaces for family activities, and modelling healthy digital habits as parents and caregivers. It also entails fostering open communication and collaboration within the family, creating opportunities for meaningful connection and shared experiences that strengthen bonds and promote a sense of belonging.

Ultimately, the impact of excessive screen time on family bonding cannot be overstated. As parents and caregivers, it's essential to be mindful of the potential consequences and to prioritize quality time spent together as a family. By striking a balance between screen time and other activities, we can preserve the sanctity of family bonding and create lasting memories that nourish the soul and enrich the fabric of our family lives.

Strategies to Mitigate Adverse Effects and Foster Well-being:

Structured Screen time:

In navigating the challenges posed by increased screen time, efficient parenting necessitates a multifaceted approach aimed at mitigating adverse effects and fostering overall well-being. Structured screen time emerges as a foundational strategy, offering children a clear framework within which to engage with digital devices intentionally and purposefully. By delineating specific periods for screen use, parents provide boundaries that help children understand the parameters of their digital interactions, fostering responsible engagement while promoting a healthy balance between online and offline activities.

Setting Clear Guidelines:

Clear guidelines further reinforce this structured approach, defining expectations regarding device usage, online platforms, and permissible content. By establishing a family digital contract collaboratively with children, parents not only set clear boundaries but also involve their children in the decision-making process, fostering a sense of ownership and accountability for their digital behaviour. These guidelines serve as a roadmap for navigating the complexities of the digital world, empowering children to make informed choices and exercise responsible judgment in their online interactions.

Promoting Online Safety Practices:

Central to efficient parenting is the promotion of online safety practices, wherein children are educated about the importance of safeguarding personal information, recognizing inappropriate content, and responding to cyber bullying. Regular check-ins provide opportunities for open dialogue about technology usage, enabling parents to gain insights into their children's digital experiences and offer guidance and support as needed. Additionally, parents must remain vigilant for signs of cyber bullying and provide a supportive environment wherein children feel comfortable sharing their online concerns and experiences.

Responsible Modelling:

Modelling responsible digital behaviour is paramount, as parents serve as powerful role models for their children. By practicing good online etiquette, managing screen time effectively, and demonstrating a healthy balance between virtual and real-world activities, parents instill valuable lessons in digital citizenship and responsible technology use.

Leveraging parental control tools further enhances parents' ability to monitor and manage their children's online activities while respecting their need for autonomy and privacy.

Digital Literacy:

Efficient parenting also involves fostering digital literacy, equipping children with the knowledge and skills necessary to navigate the digital landscape responsibly. By educating children about the implications of their digital actions and promoting critical thinking and discernment in virtual spaces, parents empower their children to make informed decisions and engage with technology mindfully. Moreover, promoting outdoor activities and diversifying offline interests helps counteract the sedentary nature of screen time, fostering holistic well-being and promoting a balanced lifestyle.

Establishing Tech-free Zones:

Establishing tech-free zones and times within the household ensures that family bonding remains uninterrupted and prioritizes face-to-face interaction. By encouraging regular conversations, shared meals, and recreational activities, parents cultivate a sense of connection and strengthen familial bonds. Parental engagement in non-screen activities further reinforces this emphasis on balance, setting a positive example for children to emulate.

Efficient parenting in the digital age requires a proactive and balanced approach that acknowledges the risks of increased screen time while leveraging strategies to mitigate adverse effects and promote overall well-being. By implementing these strategies thoughtfully and engaging in open dialogue with their children, parents can transform screen time into a tool for positive growth, enhanced family bonding, and the cultivation of healthy digital habits.

"The most incredible adventures are often the ones,
Created in the minds of children"

1.2 The Tightrope of Individuality Vs. Societal Expectations:

Nurturing Unique Paths amid Societal Expectations:

One of the most challenging waltzes in case of efficient parenting involves navigating the overwhelming societal pressures that parents often encounter. The expectation to conform to societal norms can feel like a relentless undertow, pulling parents in conflicting directions. This pressure often manifests in a desire for academic achievements, predefined career trajectories, and a particular social status. Understanding and addressing this pressure is integral to efficient parenting, as the stifling weight of conformity can lead parents to project their own unfulfilled ambitions onto their children. Striking the delicate balance between fostering individuality and meeting external benchmarks of success becomes a tightrope walk. This delicate dance occurs simultaneously with societal expectations that often prescribe specific paths to success. Striking the right balance is a nuanced challenge, as the desire to let children chart their own course can clash with prevailing societal norms. Efficient parenting, in this context, is about setting realistic expectations that allow children to flourish at their own pace.

The Dilemma of Conventional Success:

1. Academic Achievements:

The pursuit of academic achievement has long been ingrained in societal norms, often serving as a benchmark for success and fulfilment. In many cultures, parents, influenced by these expectations, may place a significant emphasis on their children's academic performance, viewing high grades, accolades, and admission to prestigious institutions as the ultimate measures of success. However, this relentless pursuit of academic excellence can have far-reaching implications for children's well-being, often overshadowing their mental health and stifling their true passions and interests.

One of the primary challenges associated with the societal emphasis on academic achievements is the pressure it places on children to excel academically, sometimes at the expense of their mental well-being. The relentless pursuit of high grades and academic accolades can create an environment of intense competition and perfectionism, leading to heightened levels of stress, anxiety, and burnout among children. Moreover, the fear of failure and the pressure to meet unrealistic expectations can take a toll on children's self-esteem and confidence, leading to feelings of inadequacy and self-doubt.

The emphasis on academic achievement may inadvertently discourage children from exploring their true passions and interests. In the pursuit of academic success, children may feel compelled to prioritize subjects and activities that are deemed "valuable" or "practical" by societal standards, rather than pursuing activities that bring them joy and fulfilment. This can lead to a sense of disconnection from their authentic selves and a lack of enthusiasm for learning, ultimately undermining their intrinsic motivation and sense of purpose.

The relentless focus on academic achievements may contribute to a narrow definition of success, wherein children's worth and value are measured solely by their academic performance. This can create undue pressure on children to conform to societal expectations and standards, leading to feelings of anxiety, stress, and burnout. Additionally, the emphasis on academic success may overshadow other important aspects of children's development, such as creativity, critical thinking, and emotional intelligence, which are equally essential for their long-term success and well-being.

Efficient parenting involves striking a balance between supporting children's academic pursuits and nurturing their overall well-being and holistic development. It entails fostering a growth mind-set, wherein children are encouraged to embrace challenges, learn from setbacks, and pursue their passions with enthusiasm and resilience. Moreover, efficient parenting involves cultivating a supportive and nurturing environment wherein children feel valued and accepted for who they are, regardless of their academic achievements.

Furthermore, efficient parenting involves helping children develop a healthy perspective on academic success, wherein they understand that grades and accolades are not the sole determinants of their worth or potential. It involves encouraging children to pursue their interests and passions, explore diverse opportunities for learning and growth, and celebrate their achievements and successes, however big or small. By fostering a holistic approach to education and embracing children's individual strengths and talents, parents can empower their children to thrive academically and personally, while also nurturing their overall well-being and happiness.

2. Predetermined Career Trajectories:

In many societies, there exists a pervasive narrative that defines certain career paths as markers of success and prestige. Whether it's becoming a doctor, lawyer, engineer, or pursuing a career in finance or technology, these predetermined trajectories are often upheld as the epitome of achievement. As a result, children may feel pressured to conform to these societal expectations, foregoing their authentic interests and talents in favour of pursuing careers that are deemed socially acceptable or prestigious.

One of the primary challenges associated with predetermined career trajectories are the pressure they place on children to follow a narrow and predefined path. From a young age, children may be influenced by societal messages that equate success with specific professions or industries, leading them to internalize these expectations and shape their aspirations accordingly. As a result, children may feel compelled to pursue careers that align with these predetermined trajectories, even if they lack genuine interest or passion for the field.

Moreover, the pressure to conform to predetermined career trajectories can stifle children's creativity, innovation, and personal growth. By limiting children's options and imposing rigid expectations, society may inadvertently discourage them from exploring alternative career paths or pursuing unconventional interests. This can hinder their ability to discover and develop their unique talents and passions, ultimately depriving them of the opportunity to pursue fulfilling and meaningful careers that align with their authentic selves.

It may also contribute to a lack of diversity and innovation in the workforce. When children are encouraged to follow conventional career paths dictated by societal norms, it can lead to a homogenization of talent and a limited range of perspectives and ideas in the workforce. This not only stifles innovation and creativity but also perpetuates existing inequalities and biases within society.

Efficient parenting involves empowering children to explore their interests, passions, and talents, free from the constraints of predetermined career trajectories. It entails fostering a supportive and nurturing environment wherein children feel encouraged to pursue their own unique paths and follow their dreams, regardless of societal expectations. This may involve exposing children to a diverse range of career options and opportunities, encouraging them to explore different fields and industries, and providing guidance and support as they navigate their career journeys.

It involves helping children develop a strong sense of self-awareness and self-confidence, enabling them to make informed decisions about their career paths based on their own values, interests, and strengths. This may involve encouraging children to reflect on their passions, values, and goals, and empowering them to pursue careers that align with their authentic selves, rather than conforming to external expectations.

Ultimately, efficient parenting involves supporting children in forging their own paths and realizing their full potential, regardless of societal pressures or predetermined career trajectories. By fostering a culture of creativity, curiosity, and self-expression, parents can empower their children to pursue fulfilling and meaningful careers that bring them joy, purpose, and fulfilment in life.

3. Social Status:

The pursuit of societal success often intertwines with the desire to attain a particular social status, which serves as a visible marker of accomplishment and recognition within one's community or social circles. In many societies, there exists an implicit understanding that certain achievements or markers of success, such as prestigious careers, material wealth, or membership in exclusive social groups, confer a higher social status upon individuals and their families. Consequently, parents may find themselves ensnared in the trap of wanting their children to conform to these predetermined moulds, striving to secure recognition and approval within their social circles.

One of the primary challenges associated with the pursuit of social status is the pressure it places on children to conform to societal expectations and norms. From a young age, children may internalize the message that their worth and value are contingent upon their ability to achieve certain milestones or benchmarks of success. As a result, they may feel compelled to pursue paths that align with these societal expectations, even if it means sacrificing their own dreams, passions, or values in the process.

Moreover, the pursuit of social status can create a culture of comparison and competition within families and communities, wherein individuals are constantly striving to outdo one another in terms of achievements, possessions, or outward displays of success. This can foster feelings of insecurity, inadequacy, and anxiety among children, as they grapple with the pressure to measure up to unrealistic standards and ideals set by society.

Furthermore, the pursuit of social status may perpetuate inequalities and divisions within society, as individuals and families vie for limited resources, opportunities, and privileges. Those who are unable to attain or maintain a certain social status may experience feelings of exclusion, marginalization, and shame, further exacerbating existing disparities and inequities within society.

Efficient parenting involves helping children develop a healthy and balanced perspective on social status, wherein they understand that true worth and fulfilment come from within, rather than external markers of success or recognition. It entails fostering a supportive and nurturing environment wherein children feel accepted and valued for who they are, regardless of their social standing or achievements.

Moreover, efficient parenting involves encouraging children to cultivate authentic connections and relationships based on mutual respect, empathy, and shared values, rather than superficial measures of status or prestige. This may involve modelling positive social behaviours and attitudes, teaching children the importance of kindness, empathy, and inclusivity in their interactions with others.

Ultimately, efficient parenting involves empowering children to define success on their own terms and pursue paths that align with their own values, interests, and passions, rather than conforming to external expectations or societal pressures. By fostering a sense of self-awareness, confidence, and resilience in children, parents can help them navigate the complexities of social status and find fulfilment and happiness in life, irrespective of their position within society. Addressing the pursuit of conformity in parenting is not about rejecting societal norms outright but about navigating them with a nuanced understanding of individual needs and aspirations. Parents can guide their children towards a path that aligns with their authentic selves, fostering a sense of fulfilment and purpose. It is a blend of understanding, support, and proactive encouragement. Nurturing of unique paths with the acknowledgment of societal expectations. It seeks to harmonize an environment where children can confidently express their individuality and embark on journeys that align with their authentic selves.

4. Redefining Success:

Redefining success lies at the core of efficient parenting, prompting a critical reassessment of societal norms and encouraging children to define success on their own terms. In navigating this journey, parents confront a clash between nurturing their children's individuality and the pressures imposed by societal expectations, which often prescribe specific benchmarks of achievement. This tension stems from established norms that dictate certain paths to success, such as academic excellence, lucrative careers, or material wealth. As parents grapple with this tension, they are tasked with redefining success in a way that prioritizes personal growth, happiness, and fulfilment over rigid adherence to external standards.

Efficient parenting challenges the notion of success as a one-size-fits-all concept and instead embraces the diversity of individual experiences and aspirations. It involves empowering children to explore their unique interests, passions, and talents, irrespective of whether they align with traditional notions of success. By encouraging children to pursue paths that resonate with their authentic selves, parents foster a sense of autonomy, self-discovery, and purpose, laying the groundwork for a fulfilling and meaningful life journey.

Efficient parenting entails fostering open dialogue and communication within the family, wherein children feel supported in expressing their aspirations, dreams, and concerns. By creating a non-judgmental space for honest conversations, parents can gain insights into their children's values, priorities, and goals, enabling them to provide guidance and support that aligns with their children's individual needs and aspirations.

Redefining success also involves shifting the focus from external validation to intrinsic motivation and personal fulfilment. Instead of measuring success solely in terms of academic achievements, career advancements, or material possessions, parents encourage their children to cultivate qualities such as resilience, empathy, creativity, and adaptability. These qualities serve as the building blocks of a well-rounded and thriving individual, capable of navigating life's challenges with grace and confidence.

Furthermore, efficient parenting emphasizes the importance of celebrating progress and growth, rather than fixating on outcomes or results. By recognizing and appreciating their children's efforts, resilience, and achievements, parents instill a sense of self-worth and confidence that transcends external validation. This positive reinforcement fosters a growth mind-set, wherein children view challenges as opportunities for learning and development, rather than obstacles to be feared or avoided.

Redefining success is a fundamental aspect of efficient parenting, necessitating a critical examination of societal norms and a commitment to empowering children to define success on their terms. By challenging rigid definitions of success and embracing the diversity of individual experiences and aspirations, parents cultivate an environment where children can thrive, grow, and fulfil their potential, guided by their own unique paths and aspirations.

Efficient Strategies to Overcome Societal Pressures:

Navigating societal pressures can be challenging for parents, but here are some practical strategies to help overcome them:

1. **Clarify Your Values:** Take time to identify your core values as a parent and as a family. Knowing what matters most to you will help you stay focused and confident in your parenting decisions, even in the face of societal pressure.

2. **Educate Yourself:** Stay informed about different parenting approaches, child development, and relevant research. Understanding the science behind parenting can give you the confidence to trust your instincts and make informed choices that align with your values.

3. **Establish Boundaries:** Set clear boundaries with friends, family members, and others who may impose their beliefs or expectations on your parenting. Politely but firmly communicate your boundaries and advocate for your autonomy as a parent.

4. **Build a Support System:** Surround yourself with supportive friends, family members, or parenting groups who respect your parenting choices. Having a supportive network can provide validation, encouragement, and practical advice when facing societal pressures.

5. **Practice Self-Compassion:** Parenting is challenging, and it's okay to make mistakes or deviate from societal norms. Practice self-compassion and remind yourself that you're doing the best you can for your child. Treat yourself with kindness and understanding, especially during difficult times.

6. **Focus on Your Child:** Keep your child's well-being at the forefront of your decisions. Instead of succumbing to societal pressures, prioritize what is best for your child's physical, emotional, and social development. Trust your instincts as a parent and tune into your child's needs.

7. **Challenge Stereotypes**: Be willing to challenge societal stereotypes and expectations about parenting roles, gender norms, and family structures. Embrace diversity and celebrate the uniqueness of your family, regardless of whether it aligns with traditional norms.

8. **Lead by Example:** Model authenticity and resilience for your children. Show them that it's okay to be true to themselves and stand up for what they believe in, even when it goes against societal norms. By living your values, you teach your children to do the same.

9. **Seek Professional Guidance:** If societal pressures are significantly impacting your well-being or your ability to parent effectively, don't hesitate to seek support from a therapist, counsellor, or parenting coach. Professional guidance can provide perspective, coping strategies, and validation for your experiences.

10. **Celebrate Your Successes**: Take pride in your parenting accomplishments and celebrate the positive moments with your child. Reflect on the progress you've made as a parent and acknowledge the strength and resilience it takes to navigate societal pressures while prioritizing your child's needs.

Remember, every family is unique, and there is no one-size-fits-all approach to parenting. Trust yourself, stay true to your values, and focus on creating a loving and supportive environment where your child can thrive.

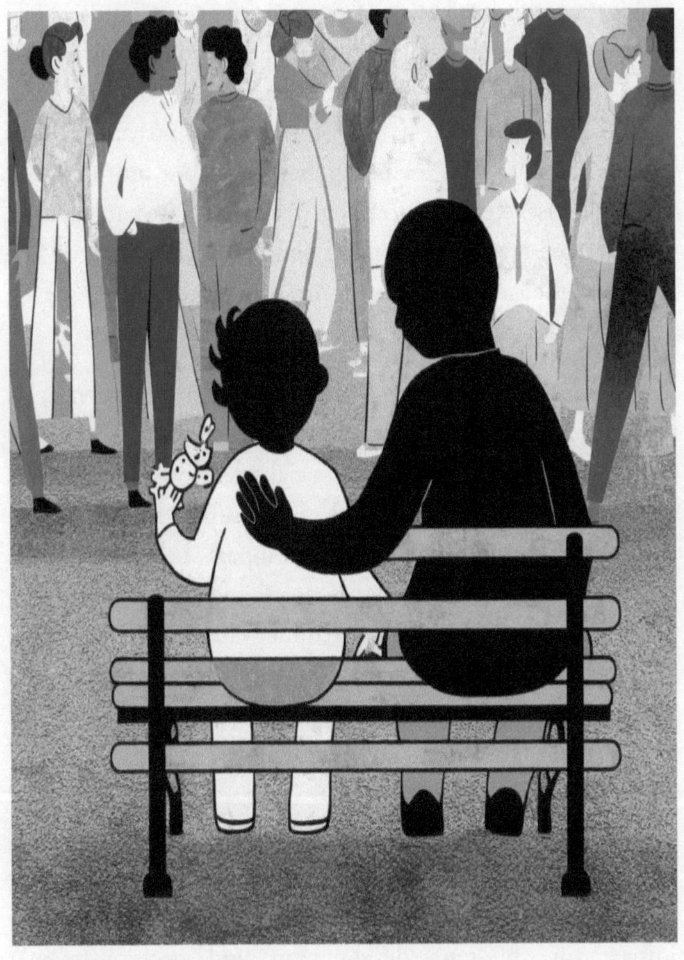

"Focus on your Child"

1.3 Peer Pressure Peaks: Guiding Through Influence in Parenting

Navigating the intricacies of peer pressure is a fundamental aspect of efficient parenting, as it represents a formidable force that significantly influences a child's development and decision-making process. Peer influence can shape various aspects of a child's life, including their behaviour, attitudes, and values. Thus, effective parenting strategies must encompass a multifaceted approach aimed at equipping children with the necessary tools to navigate peer pressure successfully, fostering resilience, and nurturing a strong sense of self-identity.

Peer pressure peaks during childhood and adolescence, as children begin to seek validation and acceptance from their peers while establishing their social identity. This pressure can manifest in various forms, from subtle suggestions to outright coercion, and may encompass behaviours such as conformity to social norms, experimentation with risky activities, or engagement in harmful behaviours. In the face of these challenges, parents play a critical role in guiding their children through the peaks of peer pressure, providing them with support, guidance, and mentorship.

Understanding Peer Pressure:

Peer pressure is a multifaceted phenomenon that encompasses both positive and negative influences, exerting a significant impact on children's development and decision-making processes. Understanding the dynamics of peer pressure is crucial for efficient parenting, as it enables parents to support their children in navigating the complexities of social interactions and making informed choices.

- **Positive and Negative Influences:** Peer pressure can manifest in various forms, ranging from positive encouragement to negative coercion. Positive peer pressure occurs when peers influence each other to engage in behaviours that promote personal growth, well-being, and positive social interactions. For example, a child may be encouraged by peers to participate in extracurricular activities, volunteer work, or academic pursuits, leading to enhanced self-esteem and skill development. On the other hand, negative peer pressure involves behaviours or attitudes that may be harmful, risky, or contrary to the child's values and goals. This can include activities such as substance abuse, bullying, or delinquent behaviour, which may have detrimental effects on the child's well-being and development. Efficient parenting involves helping children distinguish between positive and negative influences, empowering them to make choices that align with their values and aspirations.

- **Impact on Self-Identity:** Peer pressure often plays a pivotal role in shaping a child's self-identity and sense of belonging. The desire to fit in and be accepted by peers can sometimes lead children to compromise their authentic selves or engage in behaviours that are inconsistent with their values. This phenomenon is particularly pronounced during adolescence, a period characterized by heightened social sensitivity and a strong need for peer approval. Efficient parenting aims to empower children to develop a strong sense of self amidst external influences, fostering confidence, self-esteem, and resilience. By nurturing open communication, encouraging self-reflection, and providing positive reinforcement, parents can help their children navigate peer pressure while staying true to their values and beliefs. Additionally, parents can support their children in cultivating diverse social connections and friendships based on mutual respect, trust, and shared interests, thereby reducing the influence of negative peer pressure and promoting positive peer interactions.

Efficient Parenting Strategies for Peer Pressure:

Efficient parenting strategies for addressing peer pressure are vital for guiding children through the complexities of social interactions and empowering them to make informed choices. Here, we explore these strategies in detail, providing insights and practical tips for parents seeking to support their children in navigating peer pressure effectively:

- **Build Open Communication:** The cornerstone of efficient parenting in addressing peer pressure lies in fostering open communication within the family. Create a safe and supportive environment where children feel comfortable sharing their thoughts, experiences, and concerns without fear of judgment. Regularly engage in conversations about peer interactions to stay informed about their social dynamics and provide guidance when needed. By establishing open lines of communication, parents can gain valuable insights into their children's lives and offer support and advice when navigating peer pressure situations.
- **Teach Critical Thinking:** Equip children with critical thinking skills to evaluate the consequences of their

actions and decisions. Efficient parenting involves fostering a mind-set that encourages thoughtful reflection on the potential outcomes of succumbing to peer pressure versus staying true to oneself. Encourage children to consider the long-term implications of their choices and to weigh the risks and benefits before making decisions. By empowering children with critical thinking skills, parents enable them to make informed choices and resist negative influences.

- **Encourage Individuality:** Efficient parenting involves fostering an appreciation for individuality within the family. Encourage children to embrace their unique qualities, interests, and values, instilling a sense of confidence that acts as a powerful shield against conformity driven by peer pressure. Celebrate diversity and encourage children to express themselves authentically, fostering a strong sense of self-identity and resilience in the face of external pressures to conform.

- **Set Clear Expectations:** Establish clear expectations regarding behaviour and values within the family. Clearly communicate the family's values and the importance of making decisions aligned with those values. By setting clear expectations, parents provide children with a solid foundation when faced with conflicting influences from peers. Reinforce the importance of integrity, empathy, and respect in all interactions, and encourage children to uphold these values even in challenging situations.

- **Role Model Resilience:** Parents serve as influential role models for their children. Demonstrate resilience in the face of challenges and showcase the strength to resist negative influences. Efficient parenting involves modelling behaviours that reflect a steadfast commitment to personal values, even in the face of peer pressure. By demonstrating resilience and integrity in their own actions, parents inspire and empower their children to do the same.

- **Support Peer Relationships**: Foster positive peer relationships by encouraging friendships that align with the family's values. Efficient parenting involves guiding children towards friendships that promote growth, mutual respect, and shared values, acting as a counterforce to negative peer pressure. Encourage children to surround themselves with supportive and positive influences, and provide guidance on how to navigate peer relationships effectively. By supporting healthy peer relationships, parents can help children develop a strong support network and resist negative peer pressure more effectively.

By equipping children with the tools and guidance they need to navigate peer pressure effectively, parents empower them to make informed choices, uphold their values, and develop resilience in the face of external influences.

Practical Solutions for Parents:

Navigating peer pressure can be challenging for both parents and children, but with practical solutions and proactive strategies, parents can effectively support their children in facing these challenges. Here are detailed insights into practical solutions for parents to address peer pressure:

- **Scenario Role-Playing:** Engage in scenario role-playing exercises with children to help them practice assertive responses to potential peer pressure situations. This hands-on approach allows children to develop effective strategies for resisting negative influences in a safe and supportive environment. By simulating various scenarios, parents can empower children to assert their boundaries, communicate their values confidently, and make informed decisions when faced with peer pressure.

- **Offer Guidance, Not Judgment:** When discussing peer pressure experiences, it's essential for parents to offer guidance and support rather than passing judgment. Creating a non-judgmental space encourages children to share their struggles and seek guidance without fear of retribution or criticism. By approaching conversations with empathy and understanding, parents can build trust and strengthen their connection with their children, making it easier for children to confide in them about their experiences and concerns.

- **Facilitate Group Discussions:** Encourage group discussions among siblings or with trusted friends about the challenges of peer pressure. Sharing experiences in a supportive environment helps children realize they are not alone in facing these challenges and provides opportunities for peer support and encouragement. By facilitating group discussions, parents can create a sense of camaraderie and solidarity among children, empowering them to navigate peer pressure collectively.

- **Monitor Social Media Engagement:** In the digital age, monitoring children's social media engagement is essential for understanding the dynamics of their online peer interactions. Efficient parenting involves staying informed about potential pressures exerted through online platforms and being aware of any concerning behaviours or trends. By maintaining open communication about online activities and setting clear boundaries around social media usage, parents can help mitigate the negative effects of peer pressure in the digital realm.

- **Involve School Resources**: If necessary, involve school resources such as counsellors or teachers to address peer pressure concerns. Efficient parenting extends beyond the home, collaborating with educational institutions to create a supportive network for children. School counsellors and teachers can offer additional support, guidance, and resources to help children navigate peer pressure effectively and develop resilience skills. By working together with school professionals, parents can ensure that their children receive comprehensive support in managing peer pressure both inside and outside the classroom.

By implementing these proactive strategies and maintaining open communication with their children, parents can empower them to navigate peer pressure with confidence, resilience, and integrity, ultimately fostering their social and emotional well-being.

"Play is the highest form of research."
"Childhood is a journey, not a race. Allow your children to have time to explore, to play, and to learn."

1.4 The Multitasking Maze: Balancing Act in Modern Parenting

In the intricate web of modern parenting, the Multitasking Maze emerges as a significant challenge, demanding a delicate balance between various responsibilities in the fast-paced landscape of contemporary life. Parents find themselves constantly pulled in multiple directions, juggling the demands of work, family, and personal pursuits. This multitasking frenzy can often feel overwhelming, leaving parents struggling to maintain a sense of equilibrium amidst competing priorities.

Efficient parenting in the face of the Multitasking Maze requires a strategic approach that prioritizes balance and harmony across all aspects of life. It involves recognizing and acknowledging the demands of each role – as a parent, a professional, and an individual – and finding ways to fulfil these responsibilities without sacrificing one for the other. This entails cultivating time management skills, setting clear boundaries, and establishing routines that allow for effective multitasking while also ensuring adequate time for rest, relaxation, and self-care.

Navigating the Multitasking Maze calls for effective communication and collaboration between parents, partners, and support networks. By sharing responsibilities and coordinating schedules, parents can alleviate some of the burdens associated with multitasking; creating a support system that enables them to navigate the complexities of modern parenting more effectively. This collaborative approach fosters a sense of teamwork and solidarity, allowing parents to lean on each other for guidance, encouragement, and assistance when needed.

Efficient parenting strategies for managing the Multitasking Maze involve embracing flexibility and adaptability in the face of unexpected challenges and disruptions. Despite meticulous planning and organization, life often throws curveballs that can derail even the most well-laid plans. By remaining flexible and resilient, parents can navigate these obstacles with grace and composure, adjusting their strategies as needed to maintain balance and stability in their lives.

In addition, efficient parenting in the Multitasking Maze requires mindfulness and presence in each moment, rather than succumbing to the pressures of multitasking and constant distraction. By practicing mindfulness techniques and being fully present with their children, parents can cultivate deeper connections and foster a sense of intimacy and trust within the family unit. This intentional focus on quality over quantity allows parents to make the most of their time together, creating meaningful memories and experiences that enrich the parent-child relationship.

The Multitasking Maze presents a formidable challenge for modern parents, demanding a delicate balance between competing priorities and responsibilities. Efficient parenting strategies for navigating this complex terrain involve prioritizing balance, effective communication, flexibility, and mindfulness. By embracing these principles, parents can successfully navigate the Multitasking Maze and create a harmonious and fulfilling family life amidst the chaos of contemporary living.

Challenges in Balancing Work, Family, and Personal Life:

1. Overlapping Responsibilities:

The concept of Overlapping Responsibilities emerges as a significant challenge, presenting parents with a complex array of duties and obligations that often intersect and compete for their attention. This challenge is magnified by the multifaceted nature of contemporary life, where parents must navigate a myriad of roles and responsibilities, ranging from professional commitments to familial duties and personal aspirations.

One of the primary challenges associated with overlapping responsibilities is the sheer volume and diversity of tasks that parents must manage simultaneously. In today's fast-paced world, parents often find themselves pulled in multiple directions, juggling the demands of their careers, household responsibilities, childcare duties, and personal pursuits. This constant juggling act can be overwhelming, leaving parents feeling stretched thin and struggling to maintain a sense of balance and harmony in their lives.

The challenge of overlapping responsibilities is compounded by the inherent tension between these different spheres of life. For example, the demands of a demanding career may clash with the desire to spend quality time with family, while personal aspirations may take a backseat to the immediate needs of childcare and household management. This tension can create feelings of guilt, frustration, and inadequacy as parents strive to meet the expectations and obligations associated with each role.

Efficient parenting in the face of overlapping responsibilities requires a strategic approach that prioritizes effective time management, delegation, and boundary-setting. Parents must learn to identify their most critical priorities and allocate their time and energy accordingly, focusing on tasks that align with their values, goals, and long-term aspirations. This may involve establishing clear boundaries between work and home life, setting aside dedicated time for family activities, and learning to say no to non-essential commitments.

Efficient parenting strategies for managing overlapping responsibilities involve fostering open communication and collaboration within the family unit. By sharing responsibilities and coordinating schedules, parents can lighten the load and create a more balanced and harmonious household environment. This collaborative approach also fosters a sense of teamwork and solidarity, strengthening family bonds and promoting a sense of shared purpose and responsibility.

Additionally, efficient parenting requires a commitment to self-care and personal well-being. In the midst of managing overlapping responsibilities, parents must prioritize their own health and happiness, ensuring that they have the energy and resilience to meet the demands of their various roles. This may involve setting aside time for relaxation, exercise, and self-reflection, as well as seeking support from friends, family, or professional resources when needed.

The challenge of overlapping responsibilities is a central feature of modern parenthood, demanding a strategic and intentional approach to time management, delegation, and boundary-setting. By prioritizing effective communication, collaboration, and self-care, parents can successfully navigate the complexities of overlapping responsibilities and create a more balanced and fulfilling family life.

2. Time Constraints:

Time Constraints emerge as a formidable challenge, casting a shadow over parents' ability to balance work obligations, family responsibilities, and personal aspirations within the limited hours of each day. This scarcity of time transforms into a precious commodity, forcing parents to make difficult choices and sacrifices as they strive to fulfil their myriad roles and obligations.

One of the primary challenges associated with time constraints is the constant pressure to juggle competing priorities within a finite amount of time. From managing demanding work schedules to attending to the needs of children and maintaining relationships with partners, extended family members, and friends, parents often find themselves stretched thin, struggling to allocate their time and energy effectively. This relentless juggling act can lead to feelings of overwhelm, stress, and burnout, as parents attempt to navigate the complexities of modern life while striving to meet the needs of their families and themselves.

The challenge of time constraints is compounded by the ever-increasing demands of modern life, where technological advancements and societal expectations have blurred the boundaries between work and personal life. The proliferation of smartphones, email, and social media has created a culture of constant connectivity, where parents are expected to be available and accessible around the clock, even during supposed "downtime." This lack of separation between work and personal life further exacerbates feelings of time scarcity, leaving parents feeling as though they are always "on" and never truly able to unwind or disconnect.

Efficient parenting in the face of time constraints requires a strategic approach that prioritizes time management, boundary-setting, and self-care. Parents must learn to identify their most critical priorities and allocate their time and energy accordingly, focusing on tasks and activities that align with their values, goals, and long-term aspirations. This may involve establishing clear boundaries between work and personal life, setting aside dedicated time for family activities and self-care, and learning to delegate tasks or say no to non-essential commitments.

Furthermore, efficient parenting strategies for managing time constraints involve fostering a culture of efficiency, organization, and effective communication within the family unit. By implementing routines, schedules, and systems that streamline household management and promote collaboration, parents can optimize their use of time and create a more balanced and harmonious family life. This may include involving children in age-appropriate chores and responsibilities, coordinating schedules and activities with partners, and setting aside regular time for family meetings to discuss priorities and plans.

Additionally, efficient parenting requires a commitment to self-care and personal well-being, as parents cannot pour from an empty cup. In the midst of managing time constraints, it is essential for parents to prioritize activities that promote relaxation, rejuvenation, and mental health, such as exercise, hobbies, and spending quality time with loved ones. By taking care of themselves, parents can replenish their energy reserves and approach their responsibilities with renewed vigour and resilience.

The challenge of time constraints is a central feature of modern parenthood, demanding a strategic and intentional approach to time management, boundary-setting, and self-care. By prioritizing effective communication, organization, and personal well-being, parents can successfully navigate the complexities of time constraints and create a more balanced and fulfilling family life.

Practical Solutions for Parents:

Practical solutions for parents navigating the challenges of the multitasking maze offer actionable steps and strategies to help maintain balance and efficiency amidst competing demands. Here, we explore these solutions in detail, providing practical tips and insights for parents seeking to optimize their time and energy:

- **Establish a Weekly Planner:** Creating a weekly planner serves as a cornerstone for effective time management. Designate specific time slots for work-related tasks, family commitments, and personal activities. This visual guide helps in organizing priorities and ensuring a balanced approach to daily life. By mapping out the week ahead, parents can proactively allocate their time and resources, minimizing the risk of neglecting any particular aspect of their responsibilities.

- **Establishing Priorities:** The foundation of efficient parenting lies in discerning priorities. This involves a thoughtful examination of what matters most in each realm of life—be it work, family, or personal endeavours. By identifying these critical aspects, parents can allocate their time and energy more effectively, ensuring that they align their actions with their core values and goals.

- **Time Blocking and Scheduling:** Implementing time-blocking techniques and creating structured schedules can be instrumental in managing competing demands. By allocating dedicated time slots for work, family, and personal activities, parents can enhance productivity, minimize distractions, and maintain a sense of balance in their lives.

- **Setting Boundaries:** Efficient parenting necessitates the establishment of clear boundaries to delineate between different spheres of life. Setting limits on work-related activities during family time, and vice versa, helps maintain focus and prevent one aspect from encroaching upon the other. Communicating these boundaries with colleagues and family members fosters understanding and cooperation, ensuring mutual respect for each other's time and priorities.

- **Embracing Flexibility:** Parenthood is inherently unpredictable, requiring parents to adapt to unforeseen circumstances with grace and resilience. Efficient parenting involves embracing flexibility and adopting a mind-set that acknowledges the need to pivot and adjust plans in response to changing situations. This adaptive approach enables parents to navigate challenges without compromising overall balance and well-being.

- **Delegating Responsibilities:** Recognizing the value of delegation is crucial in managing the demands of parenthood. Efficient parenting involves involving partners, family members, or support networks in sharing responsibilities. Delegating tasks not only lightens the load for parents but also promotes collaboration and teamwork, leading to a more sustainable and harmonious family dynamic.

- **Quality over Quantity:** Efficient parenting prioritizes the quality of interactions over sheer quantity. Rather than focusing solely on the amount of time spent with work or family, parents should strive to make each moment meaningful and impactful. Prioritizing focused, intentional time fosters deeper connections and enhances the overall quality of relationships.

- **Self-Care as a Priority:** Balancing the demands of work, family, and personal life requires recognizing the importance of self-care. Efficient parenting strategies include prioritizing time for personal well-being, whether it's through exercise, hobbies, or simply taking moments for relaxation and rejuvenation. By prioritizing self-care, parents can replenish their energy reserves, reduce stress, and maintain resilience amidst the challenges of parenthood.

- **Communicate Expectations:** Open communication is essential for managing expectations both professionally and personally. Take the initiative to communicate with employers, family members, and oneself about priorities, deadlines, and boundaries. Clearly articulating expectations fosters understanding and collaboration, reducing misunderstandings and conflicts that may arise due to conflicting demands. By setting realistic expectations and boundaries, parents can navigate the multitasking maze more effectively, ensuring a smoother and more harmonious family life.

- **Leverage Technology Wisely:** Technology can be a valuable tool in streamlining time management and organization. Utilize scheduling apps, reminders, and digital calendars to keep track of appointments, deadlines, and tasks. These technology tools serve as helpful allies in managing multiple responsibilities, providing timely reminders and notifications to stay on track. By leveraging technology wisely, parents can enhance their efficiency and productivity, freeing up valuable time for meaningful interactions with family and personal pursuits.

- **Regular Check-Ins:** Schedule regular check-ins with oneself and family members to assess the effectiveness of balancing strategies. Take time to reflect on what's working well and what could be improved. Solicit feedback from family members about their needs and preferences, and be open to making adjustments as needed. These regular check-ins ensure that parents stay attuned to the evolving dynamics of family life and can make proactive changes to maintain balance and harmony. By fostering a culture of continuous improvement, parents can refine their multitasking skills and optimize their parenting journey.

Efficient parenting in the face of the multitasking maze requires a strategic and intentional approach that prioritizes what truly matters. By establishing priorities, implementing practical solutions, fostering open communication, and valuing self-care, parents can navigate the complexities of modern parenthood with greater ease and confidence. By striking a harmonious blend between work, family, and personal life, parents can create a more fulfilling and sustainable parenting journey for themselves and their families.

"The best thing you can spend on your kids is your Time."

Chapter 2

Establishing a Positive Environment

2.1 Effective communication:

Effective communication with kids is paramount for fostering strong and nurturing parent-child relationships. By creating a positive environment through communication, parents lay the foundation for trust, understanding, and mutual respect, which are essential for healthy development and emotional well-being. Several key elements contribute to effective communication with kids, each playing a pivotal role in fostering open and meaningful interactions:

1. Active Listening:

Active listening is a cornerstone of effective communication between parents and children, playing a crucial role in building trust, empathy, and understanding within the parent-child relationship. It involves fully concentrating on what the child is saying, understanding their perspective, responding appropriately, and remembering the information conveyed. Here's an in-depth exploration of active listening strategies that parents can employ to foster better communication with their kids:

- **Maintain Eye Contact:** Maintaining eye contact with the child during conversations demonstrates attentiveness and signals that the parent is fully engaged in what the child is saying. Eye contact also helps establish a connection and encourages the child to feel heard and valued.
- **Paraphrase or Repeat:** Paraphrasing or repeating what the child says in their own words helps ensure comprehension and clarifies any misunderstandings. This technique demonstrates to the child that the parent is actively listening and striving to understand their perspective.
- **Ask Open-Ended Questions:** Encouraging the child to provide more detailed responses by asking open-

ended questions fosters deeper communication and allows the child to express themselves more fully. Open-ended questions invite the child to share their thoughts, feelings, and experiences in their own words, promoting a sense of autonomy and empowerment.

- **Avoid Interrupting:** It's essential for parents to avoid interrupting the child while they are speaking, as this can disrupt their train of thought and inhibit open communication. Allowing the child to express themselves fully without interruption demonstrates respect for their thoughts and feelings and encourages them to communicate more openly.

- **Demonstrate Nonverbal Cues:** Nonverbal cues such as nodding, smiling, and using facial expressions can convey engagement, empathy, and understanding during conversations. These nonverbal cues reassure the child that their message is being received and understood, even without verbal confirmation.

By incorporating these active listening strategies into their interactions with their children, parents can create an environment conducive to open communication, mutual respect, and emotional connection. Active listening strengthens the bond between parents and children, fosters a deeper understanding of each other's perspectives, and lays the groundwork for healthy communication habits that endure throughout the parent-child relationship.

2. Presence and Attention:

Presence and attention are fundamental aspects of effective communication between parents and children, creating an environment conducive to meaningful connections and fostering a sense of closeness and understanding. Here's an in-depth exploration of presence and attention strategies that parents can employ to enhance communication with their children:

- **Put Away Distractions**: During conversations with their children, parents should prioritize being fully present by putting away distractions such as phones, tablets, or other electronic devices. By eliminating external distractions, parents can focus their attention entirely on the child, demonstrating their commitment to the interaction and signalling its importance.

- **Choose a Quiet and Comfortable Space:** Selecting a quiet and comfortable space for communication helps create an environment conducive to open dialogue and emotional expression. Whether it's a cosy corner of the living room or a peaceful outdoor setting, the chosen space should be free from distractions and conducive to meaningful conversation.

- **Ensure Physical Proximity:** Physical proximity plays a crucial role in conveying a sense of closeness and connection during communication. Parents should strive to maintain physical proximity to their children during conversations, whether through sitting side by side or engaging in activities together. This physical closeness fosters a sense of security and comfort, encouraging children to express themselves openly and honestly.

- **Use Affirmative Gestures:** Affirmative gestures, such as nodding, smiling, and maintaining eye contact, communicate genuine interest and engagement in the conversation. These gestures reassure the child that their words are being heard and valued, fostering trust and rapport between parent and child.

- **Be Mindful of Body Language:** Body language plays a significant role in conveying presence and attention during communication. Parents should maintain an open and inviting posture, avoiding crossed arms or other defensive gestures that may signal disinterest or detachment. By adopting a warm and welcoming demeanour, parents create a safe space for their children to express themselves freely.

By incorporating these presence and attention strategies into their interactions with their children, parents can cultivate a deeper sense of connection, understanding, and trust. Presence and attention lay the foundation for meaningful communication, strengthening the parent-child bond and fostering a supportive and nurturing relationship dynamic.

3. Empathy and Understanding:

Empathy and understanding are integral components of effective communication between parents and children, facilitating emotional connection, validation, and support. Here's a detailed exploration of empathy and understanding strategies that parents can employ to enhance communication with their children:

- **Acknowledge and Validate Emotions:** One of the most important aspects of empathy is acknowledging and validating the child's emotions without judgment. Parents should create a safe and supportive environment where children feel comfortable expressing their feelings, knowing that they will be heard and understood. Validating emotions involves recognizing the child's experiences as valid and understandable, even if they may differ from the parent's perspective.

- **Use Empathetic Statements:** Empathetic statements are powerful tools for conveying understanding and support. Phrases such as "I can imagine that must have been difficult for you" or "I understand why you feel that way" demonstrate empathy and help the child feel seen and heard. These statements convey to the child that their emotions are valid and worthy of acknowledgment, fostering a sense of connection and trust.

- **Reflect on Similar Experiences:** Parents can enhance empathy by reflecting on similar experiences they have had and sharing them with their children. By drawing parallels between their own feelings and experiences and those of their child, parents demonstrate shared understanding and solidarity. This approach helps the child feel less alone in their emotions and fosters a sense of connection and empathy.

- **Avoid Minimizing or Dismissing Emotions:** It's essential for parents to avoid minimizing or dismissing their child's emotions, even if they may seem trivial or irrational from the parent's perspective. Dismissing a child's emotions can make them feel invalidated and unheard, potentially leading to a breakdown in communication and trust. Instead, parents should strive to listen actively, validate the child's feelings, and offer support and understanding.

By incorporating these empathy and understanding strategies into their interactions with their children, parents can create a nurturing and supportive environment where open communication and emotional connection thrive. Empathy strengthens the parent-child bond, promotes a deeper understanding of each other's experiences, and fosters resilience and emotional well-being in children.

4. Non-Verbal Communication Strategies:

Nonverbal communication plays a significant role in parent-child interactions, complementing verbal communication and conveying emotions, intentions, and attitudes. Here's a detailed exploration of nonverbal communication strategies that parents can employ to enhance communication with their children:

- **Smile and Warm Facial Expressions:** A smile and warm facial expressions create a positive and welcoming atmosphere during interactions with children. Smiling communicates warmth, acceptance, and approachability, encouraging children to feel safe and comfortable expressing themselves. Parents should strive to maintain a friendly and inviting demeanour, using facial expressions to convey empathy, understanding, and encouragement.
- **Utilize Appropriate Touch:** Appropriate touch, such as a comforting pat on the back or a reassuring hug, can convey support, affection, and reassurance to children. Physical touch is a powerful form of nonverbal communication that can strengthen the parent-child bond and provide comfort during challenging moments.

Parents should be mindful of their child's comfort level with physical touch and respect their boundaries while offering gestures of affection and support.

- **Match Tone of Voice:** The tone of voice used during communication can significantly impact the message conveyed and the emotional tone of the interaction. Parents should match their tone of voice with the emotional context of the conversation, using a calm and soothing tone during moments of comfort and reassurance and a more assertive tone when setting boundaries or addressing challenging behaviours. By aligning their tone of voice with the emotional needs of the child, parents can enhance understanding and promote effective communication.

- **Pay Attention to Nonverbal Cues:** Children often communicate their feelings and emotions through nonverbal cues such as facial expressions, body language, and gestures. Parents should pay close attention to these nonverbal cues and respond accordingly, tuning into the child's emotional state and adapting their communication style as needed. By acknowledging and validating nonverbal cues, parents can demonstrate empathy, understanding, and attentiveness, fostering a deeper connection with their children.

- **Use Open Body Language:** Open body language, such as facing the child directly, maintaining eye contact, and adopting a relaxed posture, conveys openness, receptivity, and engagement. Parents should strive to create a physical environment that encourages open communication and active listening, using body language to signal their availability and willingness to connect with their children. By adopting open body language, parents can create a supportive and nurturing environment where children feel valued, heard, and understood.

By incorporating these nonverbal communication strategies into their interactions with their children, parents can enhance communication, strengthen the parent-child bond, and foster a supportive and nurturing relationship dynamic. Nonverbal communication complements verbal communication, enriching interactions with emotional depth, understanding, and connection.

5. Being Patient:

Patience is a crucial aspect of effective communication and parenting, as it involves allowing the child the necessary time and space to express themselves fully and authentically. Here's an in-depth exploration of patience strategies that parents can employ to enhance communication with their children:

- **Resist the Urge to Finish Sentences:** Parents should resist the urge to finish their child's sentences or interrupt them while they are speaking. Interrupting can convey a lack of respect for the child's thoughts and feelings and may discourage them from expressing themselves openly. Instead, parents should practice active listening and allow their child to communicate uninterrupted, giving them the opportunity to express themselves fully.
- **Give Time for Thought Collection:** It's essential to give the child time to collect their thoughts before responding, especially during moments of deep

reflection or emotional expression. Rushing the child or expecting immediate responses can create pressure and inhibit authentic communication. Parents should allow their child the space and time they need to process their thoughts and articulate them effectively, fostering a sense of ease and comfort in expressing themselves.

- **Demonstrate Tolerance During Silence:** Silence is an integral part of communication and may indicate that the child is processing their thoughts or emotions. Parents should demonstrate tolerance and patience during periods of silence, avoiding the temptation to fill the void with unnecessary chatter or prompts. Silence can provide valuable moments for reflection and introspection, allowing the child to express themselves in their own time and manner.

- **Be Patient with Emotional Expressions:** Children may express their emotions in various ways, including through tears, frustration, or anger. It's essential for parents to be patient and understanding during these emotional expressions, allowing the child to share at their comfort level. Parents should create a safe and supportive environment where children feel validated and accepted, even during moments of vulnerability or distress.

By incorporating these patience strategies into their interactions with their children, parents can create a supportive and nurturing environment where open communication and emotional expression thrive. Patience allows for the development of trust, respect, and understanding in the parent-child relationship, fostering a strong bond and promoting healthy communication dynamics.

6. Withholding Advice:

Withholding advice in parenting involves exercising restraint from providing immediate solutions or guidance to children until they have fully expressed themselves. This approach promotes active listening, fosters independence, and empowers children to explore their thoughts and emotions more deeply. Here's an in-depth exploration of strategies for withholding advice:

- **Allow the Child to Share Fully:** The first step in withholding advice is to allow the child ample space and time to share their thoughts, feelings, and concerns without interruption. Parents should adopt an attitude of attentive listening, demonstrating genuine interest and receptiveness to the child's perspective. By providing an open and non-judgmental space for expression, parents encourage children to communicate more openly and honestly.

- **Demonstrate Understanding Through Reflection:** Instead of immediately offering solutions, parents should focus on demonstrating understanding and empathy through reflective statements. Paraphrasing or summarizing the child's words helps validate their feelings and experiences, showing that their thoughts have been heard and acknowledged. Reflective listening also encourages deeper self-reflection and insight on the child's part.

- **Ask Permission Before Offering Advice:** Before jumping in with advice or solutions, parents should ask the child if they would like guidance or prefer to explore their feelings further. This empowers children to take an active role in their problem-solving process and respects their autonomy and decision-making capabilities. By seeking permission, parents show respect for the child's boundaries and preferences, fostering a sense of trust and collaboration.

- **Encourage Problem-solving through Open-Ended Questions:** Instead of providing direct answers, parents can encourage children to engage in critical thinking and problem-solving by asking open-ended questions. These questions prompt reflection, self-exploration, and consideration of alternative perspectives, empowering children to arrive at their own solutions. By guiding the conversation with thought-provoking questions, parents support the child's cognitive and emotional development while fostering independence and resilience.

By employing these strategies for withholding advice, parents can create a supportive and empowering environment where children feel heard, respected, and capable of navigating their own challenges. This approach cultivates strong communication skills, self-awareness, and problem-solving abilities in children, laying the foundation for their growth and development.

Practical Application:

- **Scenario:** Your child comes home upset after a challenging day at school.
- **Active Listening:** "It sounds like you had a tough day. Can you tell me more about what happened?"

- **Presence and Attention:** Put away any distractions, sit down with your child, and focus on their words and emotions.
- **Empathy and Understanding:** "I can imagine how that situation made you feel. It's okay to feel upset."
- **Nonverbal Communication Strategies:** Offer a comforting touch, maintain eye contact, and use a soothing tone of voice.
- **Being Patient:** Allow the child to share their experience without interrupting or rushing to provide solutions.
- **Withholding Advice:** "I'm here for you. If and when you're ready, we can talk about how to handle similar situations in the future."

Active listening is a continuous process that involves ongoing effort and commitment. By incorporating these strategies into your communication with kids, you create an environment where they feel heard, understood, and supported, contributing to the development of a positive and trusting relationship.

"Connection is a child's greatest need and an adult's greatest influence."

2.2   Creating a Judgment-Free Zone for Kids: Fostering Deep Expression

Creating a judgment-free zone for kids is essential for fostering an environment where they feel safe and supported in expressing their thoughts and emotions authentically. This nurturing space, characterized by empathy, open-mindedness, and unconditional love, plays a crucial role in children's emotional and cognitive development. Let's delve into the significance of establishing a judgment-free zone and the benefits it offers:

- **Emotional Safety and Security:** A judgment-free zone cultivates emotional safety and security for children. When kids feel confident that they won't face criticism, ridicule, or punishment for expressing themselves, they're more likely to open up about their feelings, fears, and experiences. This sense of safety encourages emotional vulnerability and honesty, enabling children to explore their inner world without fear of judgment.

- **Encourages Authentic Expression:** In a judgment-free environment, children feel free to express themselves authentically, without the pressure to conform to societal expectations or parental standards. They can share their thoughts, opinions, and experiences without filtering or censoring themselves, fostering a deeper connection with their own emotions and identity. Authentic expression promotes self-awareness, self-acceptance, and emotional intelligence in children.

- **Validation and Empathy:** When children express themselves in a judgment-free zone, they receive validation and empathy from caregivers and peers. Instead of dismissing or invalidating their feelings, adults and peers respond with understanding, compassion, and support. This validation validates children's experiences, reinforces their sense of worth and belonging, and builds trust in their relationships. Empathetic responses teach children that their feelings matter and that they are worthy of love and acceptance.

- **Promotes Healthy Communication Skills:** Establishing a judgment-free zone fosters healthy communication skills in children. They learn to express themselves articulately, assertively, and respectfully, while also listening attentively to others. These communication skills are invaluable in building positive relationships, resolving conflicts constructively, and navigating social interactions effectively. By practicing non-judgmental communication, children develop empathy, perspective-taking, and conflict resolution skills.

- **Enhances Cognitive Development:** An environment free from judgment encourages critical thinking, curiosity, and creativity in children. When kids feel safe to explore ideas, ask questions, and make mistakes without fear of criticism, they engage more actively in learning and problem-solving. This intellectual freedom stimulates cognitive development, fosters intellectual curiosity, and promotes a lifelong love of learning.

Creating a judgment-free zone for kids is crucial for nurturing their emotional well-being, promoting authentic expression, and fostering healthy relationships. By prioritizing empathy, open-mindedness, and unconditional love, caregivers and educators can create a supportive environment where children feel valued, understood, and empowered to thrive emotionally, socially, and intellectually.

Strategies to create a Judgment-free zone:

Creating a judgment-free zone within the family environment is a powerful way to foster a sense of security, trust, and emotional well-being in children. Implementing strategies that cultivate empathy, encourage open-mindedness, and communicate unconditional love can help parents establish this nurturing space where children feel free to express themselves authentically. Here are practical strategies to create a judgment-free zone:

- **Cultivating Empathy:**
  - Active Listening: Practice active listening by fully focusing on the child's words, validating their feelings, and reflecting back their emotions to demonstrate empathy and understanding.
  - Share Empathetic Stories: Share stories or examples that highlight acts of empathy and kindness, encouraging children to understand and appreciate others' perspectives.
  - Encourage Perspective-Taking: Prompt children to consider situations from different viewpoints, fostering empathy by helping them understand diverse perspectives and experiences.

- **Avoiding Criticism:**
  - Focus on Positive Aspects: Highlight the positive aspects of the child's thoughts or actions,

fostering a growth mind-set by framing feedback as opportunities for learning and improvement.

- o Constructive Feedback: Provide constructive feedback in a supportive manner, avoiding harsh criticism and instead offering guidance and encouragement for growth and development.

- **Embracing Open-Mindedness:**

  - o Model Open-Minded Behaviour: Demonstrate openness to different ideas and perspectives, expressing curiosity and a willingness to consider alternative viewpoints.
  - o Encourage Curiosity: Foster a sense of curiosity by encouraging children to ask questions and explore diverse experiences, emphasizing the value of learning from different perspectives.

- **Communicating Unconditional Love:**

  - o Express Affection: Regularly express love through both words and actions, reinforcing the idea that love is constant and unconditional, irrespective of a child's thoughts or actions.
  - o Celebrate Uniqueness: Emphasize the uniqueness of each child, communicating that their thoughts, feelings, and individuality are valued and accepted within the family.
  - o Provide Reassurance: Reassure children that they are accepted and loved for who they are, without attaching conditions to love based on their performance or behaviour.

By implementing these strategies consistently, parents can create a nurturing and supportive environment where children feel safe to express their thoughts, emotions, and concerns without fear of judgment. This judgment-free zone promotes emotional well-being, resilience, and strong communication skills, laying the foundation for healthy relationships and positive development in children.

"Behind every child who believes in himself is a parent
who believed him first."

2.3   Setting Clear Boundaries for Children:

Setting clear boundaries for children is a cornerstone of effective parenting, essential for fostering a structured environment that supports their growth, well-being, and development. Boundaries serve as guidelines that delineate acceptable behaviour, expectations, and limits within the family and broader community context. Establishing and enforcing clear boundaries requires careful consideration of various factors, including the developmental stages of children, their individual needs, and the family's values and dynamics.

Understanding Developmental Stages:

Children progress through distinct developmental stages, each characterized by unique cognitive, emotional, and social milestones. Infants and toddlers are in the early stages of development, where boundaries primarily focus on safety and physical needs. As children grow older, they move through stages such as preschool, middle childhood, and adolescence, each presenting new challenges and opportunities for boundary-setting. Parents must tailor their approach to boundary-setting to align with their child's developmental stage, considering factors such as their level of understanding, independence, and capacity for self-regulation.

Tailoring Expectations:

Effective boundary-setting involves tailoring expectations to match a child's developmental stage and individual characteristics. For example, while a pre-schooler may struggle to grasp complex rules, a teenager is capable of understanding and reasoning about more nuanced boundaries. Parents should set age-appropriate expectations that challenge and support their child's growth while considering factors such as temperament, abilities, developmental pace and any special needs or challenges they may face. Embrace and celebrate the uniqueness of each family member. Encourage tolerance and acceptance of diversity, whether it is differences in personality, interests, or backgrounds.

Establishing Consistent Rules:

Consistency is crucial when setting boundaries for children. Clear, consistent rules help children understand what is expected of them and provide a sense of predictability and security. Parents should establish rules that apply consistently across different contexts, such as home, school, and social settings, to reinforce expectations and minimize confusion. Consistency helps children internalize boundaries and develop self-discipline and responsibility. We can simplify the notion that consistency is the key in Parenting. It goes beyond being a mere rule; it becomes a guiding principle, offering a stable foundation upon which children can build their understanding of values and behaviours. Demonstrate consistency in your own behaviour. Children learn a great deal by observing, and when they see consistent actions from their parents, it reinforces the importance of sticking to established principles.

Positive Reinforcement:

Rewarding positive behaviours reinforces the value of following rules and promotes a positive environment. Consistently recognizing and praising positive actions encourages children to repeat those behaviours. Focus on the good moments, express optimism, and encourage a mind-set that embraces challenges as opportunities for growth.

Encourage Responsibility:

Gradually delegate age-appropriate responsibilities to instill a sense of accountability and independence. Where appropriate, involve children in the process of setting rules. This engagement helps them understand the reasons behind the rules and fosters a sense of responsibility for their own behaviour.

Communication and Explanation:

Effective communication is essential for successful boundary-setting. Parents should openly communicate expectations with their children, explaining the reasons behind the rules and the consequences for violating them. Using age-appropriate language and providing concrete examples help children understand the purpose and importance of boundaries. Encouraging open dialogue and allowing children to ask questions fosters mutual respect and understanding.

Enforcement and Consequences:

Enforcing boundaries requires clarity, consistency, and follow-through. Parents should establish clear consequences for violating boundaries and apply them consistently and fairly. Consequences should be appropriate to the child's age and development level, focusing on teaching lessons rather than punitive measures. Positive reinforcement for respecting boundaries can also be effective in encouraging desirable behaviour and fostering a sense of autonomy and responsibility.

Flexibility and Adaptability:

While consistency is important, parents should also be flexible and willing to adjust boundaries as needed based on changing circumstances or the child's individual needs. Flexibility allows parents to respond to unique situations and challenges while maintaining overall structure and stability. Adaptability is particularly important during transitional periods, such as starting school, moving to a new home, or experiencing significant life changes.

Family Discussions:

Hold regular family meetings to discuss any changes in rules, address concerns, and encourage open communication. This ensures that everyone is on the same page and contributes to a sense of collective responsibility. Periodically review the effectiveness of the rules and consequences. Reflect on what is working well and what may need adjustment, and involve the family in these discussions.

Setting clear boundaries for children is essential for providing structure, guidance, and support throughout their development. By considering their developmental stages, tailoring expectations, establishing consistent rules, communicating effectively, enforcing boundaries with fairness and empathy, and remaining flexible and adaptable, parents can create a nurturing environment that promotes their children's well-being, autonomy, and growth.

PARENTING

Rules without Relationship = Rebellion
Relationship without Rules = Chaos
Relationship + Rules = Respect + Responsibility

2.4   Creating a loving Atmosphere for Kids:

Creating a loving atmosphere is at the heart of efficient parenting, establishing a secure and nurturing environment for children to flourish. This atmosphere is a cornerstone for fostering emotional well-being, strengthening family bonds, and supporting positive overall development. To cultivate such an environment, express unconditional love to your children, emphasizing that their worth is not tied to behaviour or achievements but simply to who they are. Communicate love through both words and physical affection, building a sense of security and attachment. Allocate dedicated time for one-on-one interactions and engage in activities they enjoy, fostering strong emotional connections. Practice active listening, offering your full attention and responding empathetically to show that their voice is heard and valued.

Establish family traditions, whether through weekly game nights or special meals, to create a sense of belonging and shared experiences, contributing to a positive family identity. Implement consistent daily routines to provide structure and predictability, reinforcing the idea that home is a safe and loving space. Express gratitude for each family member's unique qualities and contributions, celebrating achievements big and small to encourage a positive and appreciative atmosphere.

Foster an environment where open communication is encouraged, allowing children to express thoughts and feelings without fear of judgment. Lead by example, modelling values like kindness, empathy, and respect in your interactions to guide them in navigating relationships with love and understanding. Ensure your home is both physically and emotionally safe, discouraging harsh discipline and criticism. Teach empathy, helping children understand and empathize with others' emotions, fostering compassion and kindness.

Embrace and celebrate the uniqueness of each family member, encouraging tolerance and acceptance of diversity in personality, interests, and backgrounds. Demonstrate the importance of taking responsibility for mistakes by apologizing when needed and teach the value of forgiveness, creating an atmosphere where conflicts can be resolved with love and understanding.

Encourage children's independence, allowing them the autonomy to explore and express their individuality, reinforcing their self-worth and emphasizing their value within the family. Cultivate a positive atmosphere at home by focusing on good moments, expressing optimism, and encouraging a mind-set that embraces challenges as opportunities for growth. Efficient parenting involves intentionally creating an environment where love, respect, and understanding thrive, contributing to the development of emotionally resilient and confident individuals within a loving family unit.

"The first happiness of a child is to know
that he is loved…"

"Telling your children that you love them is not a habit.
It is your constant reminder to them that they are the best
thing that has ever happened to you…"

2.5 Unconditional Love for Kids: Nurturing Emotional Well-being and Growth

Unconditional love serves as the cornerstone of a child's emotional well-being, laying the groundwork for their growth and development. It transcends behaviour or achievements, providing a safe and nurturing environment where children can flourish. Let's delve into the significance of unconditional love and practical strategies for parents to implement:

Emotional Security:

Unconditional love offers children a secure emotional base, instilling in them a sense of stability and assurance. When children know they are loved unconditionally, they develop the confidence to explore the world and face challenges head-on.

Healthy Attachment:

Consistent displays of unconditional love foster a strong bond between parent and child, promoting healthy attachment. This bond becomes a source of comfort and support, enabling children to navigate relationships with confidence and trust.

Development of Empathy:

Experiencing unconditional love teaches children empathy and compassion. By understanding that they are loved regardless of their actions, children learn to extend the same empathy to others, forming deeper connections and fostering positive relationships.

Positive Self-Image:

Unconditional love contributes to the development of a positive self-image. Children internalize the message that they are inherently valuable and worthy of love, leading to greater self-confidence and resilience in the face of challenges.

Emotional Regulation:

Children raised with unconditional love are more adept at regulating their emotions. They feel secure in expressing their feelings without fear of rejection, leading to better stress management and overall emotional well-being.

Practical Strategies for Unconditional Love:

Express Affection Regularly:

Demonstrate love through physical affection, verbal affirmations, and gestures. Make it a habit to hug your child, express your love spontaneously, and leave notes of affirmation to reinforce their sense of security and belonging.

Listen Actively:

Create a safe space for your child to express their thoughts and feelings without judgment. Dedicate focused time for one-on-one conversations, actively listening to their concerns, and showing genuine interest in their experiences.

Acknowledge Efforts, Not Just Achievements:

Celebrate your child's efforts, persistence, and willingness to try, regardless of the outcome. Emphasize the value of the learning process and growth, fostering a mind-set focused on progress rather than perfection.

Be Present in Their Lives:

Participate actively in your child's life by attending their events, engaging in activities together, and showing genuine interest in their hobbies and interests. Your presence and involvement reinforce their sense of value and significance.

Set Realistic Expectations:

Understand and accept your child's individuality, setting realistic expectations that consider their unique strengths, challenges, and developmental stage. Avoid comparing them to others and appreciate their unique qualities and contributions.

Provide Unconditional Support:

Offer unwavering support and encouragement, being their advocate and a source of comfort during both triumphs and challenges. Let your child know that you are there for them, offering guidance and reassurance without judgment.

Apologize and Forgive:

Model forgiveness and humility by acknowledging and apologizing for your mistakes. Demonstrate the importance of accepting responsibility and learning from errors, fostering a culture of openness and growth within the family.

Encourage Independence:

Foster independence by allowing your child to make age-appropriate decisions and offering guidance without imposing control. Encourage autonomy and self-reliance, empowering your child to navigate the world with confidence and resilience.

By implementing these practical strategies, parents can create a nurturing and supportive environment grounded in unconditional love, where children can thrive emotionally, socially, and cognitively.

> **"Parental love is the only love that is truly selfless, unconditional and forgiving…"**

Chapter 3

Nurturing Fundamental Life Skills in Children

3.1   Fostering Healthy Self-esteem in children:

Promoting positive self-esteem in children is pivotal for fostering their emotional well-being and overall development. A healthy sense of self-worth serves as the foundation upon which confidence, resilience, and a positive outlook on life are built. Recognizing the significance of cultivating self-esteem and employing effective strategies is key to nurturing children who grow into self-assured and emotionally resilient individuals.

Importance of Promoting Self-Esteem in Kids:

Confidence Boost:

Healthy self-esteem imbues children with a sense of confidence that empowers them to tackle challenges, voice their opinions, and approach new experiences with enthusiasm. When children believe in themselves, they are more likely to take risks and pursue their goals with determination.

Resilience Building:

A robust sense of self-worth contributes to resilience, enabling children to bounce back from setbacks and adversity. Rather than being discouraged by failures, children with healthy self-esteem view challenges as opportunities for growth, learning, and personal development.

Positive Relationships:

Self-esteem shapes how children perceive themselves in relation to others, influencing the quality of their interpersonal connections. Those with a positive self-image are more inclined to form and maintain healthy relationships, as they approach interactions from a place of self-assurance and mutual respect.

Emotional Well-Being:

The relationship between self-esteem and emotional well-being is profound. Children with positive self-esteem are better equipped to manage stress, regulate their emotions, and cultivate a healthier mental and emotional state. They exhibit greater resilience in the face of adversity and demonstrate a more optimistic outlook on life.

Academic Success:

Self-esteem significantly impacts a child's approach to learning and academic achievement. Children who possess a belief in their abilities are more likely to engage actively in the learning process, persevere through academic challenges, and strive for excellence in their academic pursuits.

Problem-Solving Skills:

Healthy self-esteem fosters effective problem-solving skills in children. When faced with obstacles, those with positive self-esteem are more inclined to approach problems with a solution-oriented mind-set, confident in their ability to overcome hurdles and find creative solutions.

Motivation and Goal Pursuit:

Self-esteem plays a pivotal role in motivating children to set and pursue goals. With a positive self-image, children are driven to achieve their aspirations, fuelled by the belief in their capability to succeed. They exhibit resilience in the face of setbacks and remain steadfast in their pursuit of personal and academic excellence.

Strategies to Promote Self-Esteem in Kids:

There are various strategies that parents and caregivers can implement to nurture self-esteem in children, fostering confidence, competence, and a healthy sense of self-worth.

- **Encouragement and Positive Reinforcement:** One effective strategy is to provide encouragement and positive reinforcement. Acknowledging and praising children for their efforts, accomplishments, and positive behaviours helps reinforce the idea that their actions are valued and appreciated. Regular expressions of genuine appreciation for their achievements can go a long way in boosting their self-esteem and motivation.
- **Supporting Individual Interests:** Supporting children's individual interests is another important aspect of promoting self-esteem. Encouraging and facilitating their exploration of activities they enjoy not only provides them with a sense of competence and accomplishment but also communicates that their interests are valued and worthy of pursuit.

- **Setting Realistic Expectations:** Setting realistic expectations is crucial for building self-esteem in children. Establishing achievable goals and expectations allows children to experience success and build confidence gradually. Breaking down tasks into manageable steps can help prevent feelings of overwhelm and foster a sense of competence and mastery.

- **Teaching Resilience:** Teaching resilience is also key to promoting self-esteem. Helping children understand that setbacks are a natural part of life and framing challenges as opportunities to learn and grow can encourage a positive mind-set and boost their confidence in their ability to overcome obstacles.

- **Effective Communication:** Effective communication plays a vital role in nurturing self-esteem in children. Creating a safe and supportive environment where children feel comfortable expressing their thoughts and feelings without fear of judgment promotes a sense of being heard and valued, contributing to their overall sense of self-worth.

- **Encouraging Decision-Making:** Encouraging decision-making and autonomy is another important strategy for promoting self-esteem. Involving children in decision-making processes and offering them opportunities to make choices reinforces their sense of competence and confidence in their decision-making abilities.

- **Modelling Positive Behaviour:** Modelling positive behaviour is also essential. Children often emulate the attitudes and behaviours they observe in significant adults, so being mindful of the language and behaviour exhibited can have a significant impact on their self-esteem and self-image.

- **Promoting a Growth Mind-set:** Promoting a growth mind-set is crucial for fostering self-esteem in children. Emphasizing the power of effort and learning, praising the process of trying, learning from mistakes, and persevering, rather than focusing solely on outcomes, encourages a positive attitude towards learning and personal growth.

- **Celebrating Diversity:** Celebrating diversity and teaching children to appreciate differences in themselves and others is another important aspect of promoting self-esteem. Fostering a sense of acceptance and inclusivity helps children develop a positive sense of self and respect for others.

- **Providing Responsibilities:** Providing children with age-appropriate responsibilities and opportunities to contribute to family responsibilities instills a sense of competence and responsibility, boosting their self-esteem and sense of worth.

- **Encouraging Peer Relationships:** Encouraging positive peer relationships and teaching children to value themselves and others within social contexts also contributes to their self-esteem and sense of belonging.

- **Establishing Healthy Boundaries:** Teaching children the importance of self-respect and healthy boundaries helps them develop a strong sense of self-worth and self-respect, fostering confidence and assertiveness in their interactions with others.

Promoting self-esteem in children is an on-going process that requires consistent support, encouragement, and positive reinforcement. By implementing these strategies, parents and caregivers can contribute significantly to the development of children who possess a strong sense of self-worth, resilience, and confidence to face the complexities of life.

Practical Solutions to Foster Self-esteem in Kids:

- **Gratitude Journal:**

    - *Activity:* Create a gratitude journal where the child can write or draw things they are thankful for each day.
    - *Objective:* Promotes a positive mind-set and appreciation for positive aspects of their life.

- **Role-Playing Confidence:**

    - *Activity:* Engage in role-playing scenarios where the child demonstrates confidence in various situations.
    - *Objective:* Boosts their self-assurance and problem-solving skills.

- **Story of Achievements:**

    - *Activity:* Create a storybook highlighting the child's achievements, big or small.
    - *Objective:* Celebrates their successes and fosters a sense of accomplishment.

- **Affirmation Mirror:**

    - *Activity:* Have the child stand in front of a mirror and say positive affirmations about themselves.

o   *Objective:* Encourages self-reflection and positive self-talk.

- **Team Building Games:**

  o   *Activity:* Engage in team-building games that require cooperation and communication.
  o   *Objective:* Boosts self-esteem through collaboration and successful teamwork.

- **Puzzle of Strengths:**

  o   *Activity:* Create a puzzle with pieces representing different strengths, and discuss each one.
  o   *Objective:* Reinforces the idea that everyone possesses unique strengths.

These activities not only enhance self-esteem but also contribute to the overall well-being of the child by fostering positive self-perception and resilience. Tailor these activities based on the child's age, preferences, and developmental stage for the most effective impact.

"Why fit-in? When you are born to stand-out?"

3.2 The Importance of Resilience in Kids: An Essential Element of Efficient Parenting

In the intricate maze of parenting, the cultivation of resilience in children emerges as a pivotal aspect. Resilience, often characterized as the ability to rebound from challenges and adversity, transcends being merely a character trait; it evolves into a skill that empowers children to navigate life's uncertainties with courage and determination. In the pursuit of efficient parenting, recognizing the significance of instilling resilience becomes paramount, as does understanding its profound impact on the holistic development of children.

Resilience as a Lifelong Asset:

Resilience is the ability to adapt and bounce back from setbacks, trauma, or stressors, and it plays a crucial role in promoting emotional well-being, mental health, and overall success in life. Here are several reasons why resilience is essential for kids:

- **Coping with Adversity**: Life is full of ups and downs, and resilience enables children to cope effectively with adversity. Whether they encounter academic setbacks, social challenges, or personal hardships, resilient children are better equipped to face obstacles head-on and overcome them.

- **Emotional Regulation:** Resilience helps children manage their emotions in healthy and constructive ways. It allows them to recognize and express their feelings, while also developing coping strategies to deal with stress, anxiety, or disappointment. By learning to regulate their emotions, children can maintain a sense of balance and well-being even in difficult situations.

- **Building Confidence and Self-Esteem:** Resilience fosters a sense of confidence and self-esteem in children. When they successfully navigate challenges and overcome obstacles, they develop a belief in their own abilities and strengths. This confidence becomes a foundation for future success and empowers children to take on new challenges with optimism and determination.

- **Promoting Problem-Solving Skills:** Resilience encourages children to approach problems and setbacks as opportunities for growth and learning. It fosters a mind-set of resilience, creativity, and resourcefulness, prompting children to seek solutions and alternatives rather than becoming overwhelmed by obstacles. This problem-solving mind-set is invaluable in both academic and real-life settings.

- **Supporting Mental Health:** Resilience is closely linked to positive mental health outcomes. Children who possess resilience are less likely to experience anxiety, depression, or other mental health issues in response to stressors or trauma. They have greater emotional stability and are better able to maintain a sense of well-being even in challenging circumstances.

- **Enhancing Social Relationships:** Resilient children tend to have stronger social connections and healthier relationships with peers, family members, and other adults. They are more adept at communicating their needs, empathizing with others, and resolving conflicts constructively. These social skills are essential for building meaningful relationships and navigating interpersonal dynamics throughout life.

- **Encouraging Perseverance and Grit:** Resilience instills qualities such as perseverance, grit, and determination in children. It teaches them the value of persistence and hard work, even in the face of setbacks or failures. By developing a resilient mind-set, children learn to persevere through challenges and setbacks, ultimately achieving their goals and aspirations.

- **Preparing for Future Challenges:** Building resilience in childhood sets the stage for future success and well-being. Life is unpredictable, and resilient children are better prepared to face the uncertainties and challenges that lie ahead. They develop the skills, attitudes, and mind-set needed to adapt, thrive, and flourish in an ever-changing world.

Strategies to build Resilience in kids:

Resilience is not only about bouncing back from difficult experiences but also about learning and growing from them. Here are several strategies to help cultivate resilience in children:

- **Promote a Growth Mind-set:** Encourage children to adopt a growth mind-set, which focuses on the belief that abilities and intelligence can be developed through effort and practice. Teach them that challenges are opportunities for growth and learning, rather than insurmountable obstacles. Praise their efforts and persistence, regardless of the outcome, to reinforce this mind-set.

- **Foster Positive Relationships:** Strong, supportive relationships with family members, friends, and other trusted adults serve as a buffer against stress and adversity. Encourage open communication and emotional expression within the family, and help children develop healthy peer relationships. Knowing they have a network of caring individuals to turn to in times of need can bolster children's resilience.

- **Encourage Problem-Solving Skills:** Teach children how to approach problems and challenges in a systematic and proactive manner. Encourage them to break down problems into manageable steps, consider various solutions, and evaluate their effectiveness. Providing opportunities for them to practice problem-solving skills builds their confidence and resilience.

- **Teach Emotional Regulation:** Help children recognize and manage their emotions effectively. Teach them coping strategies such as deep breathing, mindfulness, and positive self-talk to deal with stress and anxiety. By learning to regulate their emotions, children can approach challenges with a calmer and more composed mind-set.

- **Build Self-Efficacy:** Foster a sense of self-efficacy— the belief in one's ability to accomplish tasks and achieve goals. Encourage children to set realistic goals and work towards them gradually. Provide them with opportunities to experience success and build competence in various areas of their lives, reinforcing their belief in their own abilities.

- **Encourage Resilient Thinking:** Help children develop resilient thinking patterns by challenging negative or defeatist thoughts. Teach them to reframe setbacks as temporary and solvable, and to focus on finding solutions rather than dwelling on problems. Encourage them to identify their strengths and past successes as evidence of their ability to overcome challenges.

- **Promote Self-Care:** Teach children the importance of self-care and stress management. Encourage them to engage in activities that promote relaxation, such as exercise, hobbies, or spending time in nature. Emphasize the importance of getting enough sleep, eating healthily, and taking breaks when needed to recharge and rejuvenate.

- **Model Resilient Behaviour:** Children learn by example, so be a role model of resilience. Demonstrate positive coping strategies in your own life, and openly discuss how you overcome challenges and setbacks. By seeing resilience in action, children learn that it is possible to bounce back from adversity and grow stronger as a result.

- **Provide Opportunities for Mastery:** Give children opportunities to develop skills and talents in areas that interest them. Whether it's sports, music, art, or academics, encourage them to pursue their passions and persevere in the face of obstacles. Mastery experiences build confidence and resilience, as children learn that they can overcome challenges with effort and determination.

- **Celebrate Effort and Progress:** Focus on the process rather than the outcome when praising children's efforts. Acknowledge their hard work, perseverance, and progress, regardless of whether they achieve their goals. Celebrating small victories reinforces the idea that effort and resilience are valued and worthy of recognition.

Resilience emerges as a potent asset that shapes a child's ability to navigate the complexities of life. Efficient parenting intentionally fosters resilience, recognizing its far-reaching impact on a child's emotional well-being, social competence, and overall success in the face of life's challenges. Through strategic incorporation of resilience-promoting strategies, parents contribute significantly to the development of resilient, capable, and confident individuals who can thrive in the ever-changing landscape of the future.

"If the parents want to gift their children, the best gift they can do is to teach their children to love Challenges, be intrigued by mistakes, enjoy effort and keep on learning. That way, their children don't have to be slaves of praise. They will have a lifelong way to build and repair their own Confidence."

3.3   Encouraging Decision-Making in Children:

Encouraging decision-making in children transcends the immediate choices they encounter; it's an investment with far-reaching implications for their future. This vital life skill serves as the cornerstone for autonomy, self-assurance, and responsible adulthood. Recognizing the importance of nurturing decision-making abilities and implementing effective strategies empowers parents to cultivate children who confidently navigate life's complexities with resilience and assurance.

At its core, encouraging decision-making in children is about fostering autonomy and independence. By allowing children to make choices, parents grant them the opportunity to assert their autonomy and take ownership of their actions. This sense of self-reliance instills a mind-set where children feel capable of navigating their world and making decisions that align with their values and goals.

Decision-making is deeply intertwined with critical thinking skills. When children are encouraged to weigh different options, anticipate outcomes, and make informed choices, they develop essential problem-solving and analytical abilities. These skills are invaluable for success in academics, careers, and everyday life, enabling individuals to tackle challenges with confidence and creativity.

Decision-making teaches children the principles of responsibility and accountability. When children make decisions, they understand that their choices have consequences, whether positive or negative. This early exposure to accountability lays the groundwork for responsible behaviour, as children learn to take ownership of their actions and learn from the outcomes of their decisions.

Successful decision-making also plays a pivotal role in building confidence. As children experience the positive outcomes of their decisions, they develop a sense of self-assurance that becomes a foundation for facing challenges, pursuing goals, and embracing new opportunities throughout life. This confidence empowers them to navigate uncertain situations with poise and determination.

Furthermore, decision-making fosters adaptability and resilience. Not every decision yields the desired outcome, but through both positive and challenging consequences, children learn to adapt and persevere. This resilience becomes a valuable asset as they encounter diverse situations and setbacks, equipping them with the resilience needed to navigate life's ups and downs.

Ultimately, fostering decision-making in children is essential preparation for adulthood. The ability to make informed decisions is crucial for success in various domains, including academics, relationships, and career choices. By nurturing this skill early on, parents empower their children to confidently handle the complexities of adult life and navigate the ever-changing landscape with confidence and resilience.

Strategies to Encourage Decision-Making:

Encouraging decision-making in children can be effectively facilitated through engaging activities that stimulate their thought processes and foster independence. Here are some activities designed to promote decision-making skills in children:

- **Offer Age-Appropriate Choices:**

  - *Strategy:* Provide options that are suitable for the child's age and developmental stage.
  - *Implementation:* For younger children, this might include choices in clothing or snacks; for older children, it could involve selecting extracurricular activities.

- **Involve Them in Planning:**

  - *Strategy:* Engage children in planning activities or events.
  - *Implementation:* Let them contribute ideas for family outings or plan their own birthday celebration, encouraging them to consider various aspects.

- **Teach Decision-Making Steps:**

  - *Strategy:* Break down the decision-making process into steps.
  - *Implementation:* Teach children to identify the decision they need to make, gather information, weigh the pros and cons, and make a choice. Gradually, they can practice this process independently.

- **Encourage Problem-Solving Discussions:**

  - *Strategy:* Facilitate open discussions about problems or challenges.
  - *Implementation:* When faced with an issue, encourage children to share their thoughts on

potential solutions. Guide them in exploring different options and evaluating possible outcomes.

- **Promote Reflection After Decisions:**

  - *Strategy:* Encourage reflection on the outcomes of their decisions.
  - *Implementation:* Discuss with children what worked well and what could be improved. This reflective process enhances their ability to learn from experiences.

- **Acknowledge Their Input:**

  - *Strategy:* Acknowledge and appreciate their contributions to family decisions.
  - *Implementation:* Whether it's choosing a movie for family night or deciding on a weekend activity, recognizing their input reinforces the importance of their decision-making role.

- **Model Decision-Making:**

  - *Strategy:* Demonstrate the decision-making process through modelling.
  - *Implementation:* Let children witness how adults weigh options, consider consequences, and make decisions. This modelling provides a valuable template for their own decision-making.

- **Provide a Safe Environment for Mistakes:**

  - *Strategy:* Create an environment where mistakes are viewed as opportunities to learn.

- *Implementation:* Emphasize that not every decision will be perfect, and that's okay. Encourage a growth mind-set, where learning from mistakes is valued.

- **Build Decision-Making Gradually:**

  - *Strategy:* Start with small decisions and gradually increase complexity.
  - *Implementation:* Begin with choices like what game to play and progress to decisions about extracurricular activities or academic goals. This gradual approach builds confidence.

- **Ask Open-Ended Questions:**

  - *Strategy:* Pose questions that encourage thought and reflection.
  - *Implementation:* Instead of asking yes-or-no questions, prompt them to express their thoughts. For example, ask, "What factors do you consider when choosing your activities?"

- **Provide Information for Informed Choices:**

  - *Strategy:* Equip children with the necessary information.
  - *Implementation:* Before making decisions, ensure they have relevant details. This could be information about different subjects they want to study or the rules of a new game they want to play.

- **Celebrate Decision-Making Achievements:**

  - *Strategy:* Celebrate successful decision-making moments.

- o   *Implementation:* Whether it's choosing a new hobby or making a thoughtful choice in a challenging situation, acknowledge and celebrate their achievements.

These activities not only promote decision-making but also provide opportunities for children to learn and grow in various aspects of their lives. It's essential to adapt these activities based on the child's age, preferences, and developmental stage. Encouraging decision-making in children is an on-going process that requires patience, guidance, and a supportive environment. By instilling this crucial life skill, parents empower their children to navigate the complexities of life with confidence, resilience, and a proactive approach to challenges.

"The way kids learn to make decisions is by making decisions, not by following Directions…"

3.4   Nurturing Responsibility in Children:

Teaching responsibility to children is an integral aspect of their development, as it equips them with essential life skills that extend far beyond their formative years. By instilling a sense of responsibility, parents and educators lay the groundwork for fostering well-rounded individuals who understand the impact of their actions and actively contribute to their own well-being and that of others. Here, we delve into the importance of teaching responsibility and provide practical strategies for implementation.

Significance of Nurturing Responsibility in children:

First and foremost, teaching responsibility prepares children for life's challenges. By assigning tasks and duties, parents and educators instill a proactive mind-set, empowering children to navigate various situations with confidence. Whether it's completing chores or meeting academic deadlines, fulfilling responsibilities instills a sense of competence and readiness to tackle life's demands.

Responsibility fosters accountability in children. By taking ownership of their actions, children learn that choices have consequences. This understanding cultivates a sense of accountability, as they recognize the impact of their behaviour on themselves and others. Through this process, children develop a heightened sense of integrity and moral reasoning.

Fulfilling responsibilities also contributes to the development of self-esteem. As children successfully meet their obligations, they experience a sense of accomplishment that bolsters their self-esteem and confidence in their abilities. This positive reinforcement motivates them to take on new challenges and strive for excellence in various areas of their lives.

Additionally, teaching responsibility instills a sense of social contribution in children. Responsible individuals understand the importance of contributing to society and actively engage in activities that benefit their community. By assigning tasks that promote cooperation and collaboration, parents and educators nurture a sense of social duty and civic engagement in children from a young age.

Responsibilities often come with deadlines, requiring children to manage their time effectively. By learning to prioritize tasks and allocate time efficiently, children develop invaluable time management skills that serve them well throughout their lives. This ability to manage time effectively enables them to balance various commitments and achieve their goals with greater ease.

Fulfilling responsibilities contributes to the establishment of healthy habits that promote overall well-being. Whether it's practicing personal hygiene or maintaining an organized living space, children learn the importance of self-care and organization through their daily responsibilities. These habits lay the foundation for a healthy lifestyle and contribute to their physical and mental well-being.

In addition to practical skills, teaching responsibility enhances children's decision-making abilities. By weighing options and making choices aligned with their values, children develop critical thinking skills and learn to navigate complex decision-making processes. This ability to make informed decisions empowers them to assert control over their lives and shape their own destinies.

Furthermore, meeting responsibilities nurtures a strong work ethic in children. By understanding the effort required for achievement and success, children develop a sense of diligence and perseverance that drives them to pursue their goals with determination. This work ethic sets them up for success in academics, careers, and other pursuits.

Responsibility involves navigating conflicts and finding solutions to problems. Through the process of fulfilling their duties, children learn valuable conflict resolution skills that enable them to resolve disagreements and disputes effectively. This ability to manage conflicts constructively strengthens their interpersonal relationships and contributes to a harmonious social environment.

Finally, teaching responsibility encourages children to adopt a long-term perspective and focus on their future goals. By understanding the concept of delayed gratification and the rewards of sustained effort, children develop a sense of patience and perseverance that enables them to pursue their aspirations with resilience and determination. This long-term orientation prepares them for the challenges and opportunities that lie ahead, empowering them to achieve success and fulfilment in their lives.

Strategies for cultivating Responsibility in kids:

Teaching responsibility to children is a multifaceted endeavour that requires careful planning and implementation of effective strategies. Here, we explore various approaches to instilling a sense of responsibility in children and nurturing their development into responsible, accountable, and self-reliant individuals.

Assign Age-Appropriate Tasks:

- Start by assigning age-appropriate tasks to children. Introduce simple responsibilities gradually, considering their developmental stage and capabilities. As they grow, gradually increase the complexity of duties to challenge and expand their skills.

Lead by Example:

- Parents and caregivers play a pivotal role in modelling responsible behaviour. Children often emulate the actions of those they look up to, making it essential for adults to demonstrate responsibility in their own actions and decisions.

Establish Clear Expectations:

- Clearly communicate expectations regarding responsibilities to children. They benefit from knowing what is expected of them and understanding the reasons behind it. Clarity helps alleviate confusion and sets a clear framework for their actions.

Positive Reinforcement:

- Reinforce responsible behaviour with positive feedback. Recognition and praise for fulfilling duties encourage children to repeat responsible actions. Positive reinforcement reinforces the connection between responsible behaviour and positive outcomes.

Create a Routine:

- Establishing routines helps integrate responsibilities into daily life. Consistency fosters a sense of structure and predictability, making it easier for children to understand and fulfil their obligations.

Encourage Problem-Solving:

- Encourage children to find solutions independently when faced with challenges related to their responsibilities. Problem-solving skills are integral to responsible decision-making and promote autonomy.

Involve in Decision-Making:

- Include children in decision-making processes related to their responsibilities. This fosters a sense of autonomy and ownership, empowering them to take charge of their actions.

Discuss Consequences:

- Talk about the consequences of actions, both positive and negative. Understanding the impact of responsibilities reinforces accountability and helps children make informed choices.

Teach Organization Skills:

- Organization is a key aspect of responsibility. Teach children how to organize their belongings and manage their time effectively to fulfil their obligations efficiently.

Promote Self-reflection:

- Encourage self-reflection on completed tasks. Discuss what went well, what could be improved, and how the experience contributes to personal growth. Self-reflection fosters introspection and continuous improvement.

Create a Reward System:

- Implement a reward system tied to responsibilities. This could involve earning privileges or small incentives for consistently fulfilling duties, motivating children to take their responsibilities seriously.

Encourage Teamwork:

- Responsibilities within a family or community often involve collaboration. Encourage teamwork and cooperative efforts to achieve shared goals, fostering a sense of belonging and cooperation.

Discuss Personal Values:

- Connect responsibilities to personal values upheld by the family or community. Help children understand how their actions align with these values and contribute to the greater good.

Provide Autonomy:

- Gradually provide children with autonomy over their responsibilities. Allowing them to take charge builds a sense of ownership and fosters independence and self-reliance.

Celebrate Achievements:

- Celebrate milestones and achievements related to responsibilities. Recognition reinforces the positive impact of responsible behaviour and encourages children to continue fulfilling their duties.

Introduce Financial Responsibility:

- As children grow older, introduce financial responsibilities such as budgeting and saving money. Teach them the value of money and instill fiscal responsibility from a young age.

Encourage Initiative:

- Foster a proactive mind-set by encouraging children to take initiative in identifying and fulfilling responsibilities without constant supervision. Initiative cultivates a sense of leadership and resourcefulness.

Discuss Real-world Impact:

- Connect responsibilities to real-world impact. Discuss how individual actions contribute to the well-being of the family, community, and beyond, fostering a sense of purpose and social responsibility.

Teaching responsibility to children is a dynamic process that involves a combination of modelling, communication, and hands-on experiences. By adopting these strategies, parents and educators can play a significant role in nurturing responsible, accountable, and self-reliant individuals who carry these essential life skills into adulthood.

Activities to Teach Responsibility to Kids: Engaging and Educational

Implementing activities is a dynamic way to teach responsibility to kids. These interactive experiences not only make the learning process enjoyable but also provide practical lessons that can be applied in daily life. Here are engaging activities to instill a sense of responsibility in children:

1. Age-Appropriate Chore Chart:

- Create a colourful chore chart with age-appropriate tasks.
- Allow children to choose their responsibilities.
- Track completion and discuss the impact of contributing to household chores.

2. Personal Responsibility Journals:

- Provide each child with a personal responsibility journal.
- Encourage them to write or draw about their daily responsibilities.
- Discuss entries to promote self-reflection.

3. Decision-Making Board Game:

- Design a board game centred around making responsible decisions.
- Include scenarios and consequences, fostering decision-making skills.
- Play as a family, discussing choices and outcomes.

4. Responsibility Relay Race:

- Set up a relay race with different responsibility stations.
- Each station represents a task or responsibility to complete.
- Emphasize teamwork and communication.

5. Financial Responsibility Simulation:

- Create a mock store with play money and items for "purchase."

- Assign budgets and guide children in making responsible spending choices.
- Discuss saving and budgeting concepts.

6. Community Clean-up Day:

- Organize a community clean-up day with other families.
- Assign responsibilities like picking up trash, sorting recyclables, etc.
- Discuss the impact of maintaining a clean environment.

7. Team-building Responsibility Puzzle:

- Provide puzzle pieces with different responsibilities written on them.
- Assemble the puzzle together, discussing each responsibility.
- Emphasize the importance of each piece in completing the whole picture.

8. Personalized Responsibility Contracts:

- Develop personalized responsibility contracts with each child.
- Clearly outline duties and expected behaviour.
- Sign and display these contracts as a visual reminder.

"If you want your kids to keep theirs feet on the ground, put some responsibility on their shoulders…"

3.5   Teaching Problem solving kills for children:

Teaching problem-solving skills to children is paramount in preparing them for the complexities of life and fostering resilience and independence. This critical skill empowers children to face challenges with confidence, make informed decisions, and navigate obstacles effectively. By providing guidance, creating opportunities for practical application, and encouraging a growth mind-set, parents play a crucial role in nurturing problem-solving abilities in their children.

Understanding the Problem:

The first step in teaching problem-solving skills is helping children clearly identify the issue at hand. Encouraging them to express the problem in their own words promotes effective communication and lays the foundation for finding solutions.

Breaking Down the Problem:

Children often face complex challenges that may seem overwhelming. Teaching them to break down these problems into smaller, more manageable parts enables them to approach problem-solving systematically, reducing stress and confusion.

Generating Possible Solutions:

Encouraging children to brainstorm a range of potential solutions fosters creativity and divergent thinking. By exploring various approaches, children learn to consider multiple possibilities and develop a more nuanced understanding of problem-solving.

Considering Consequences:

An essential aspect of problem-solving is evaluating the potential outcomes of each solution. Discussing both positive and negative consequences helps children make informed decisions and understand the impact of their choices.

Decision-Making:

Guiding children in selecting the most suitable solution based on their evaluation of consequences empower them to take ownership of their decisions. Reinforcing the idea that decision-making is a skill that improves with practice encourages children to trust their judgment.

Implementing the Chosen Solution:

Supporting children in putting their chosen solution into action instills confidence and reinforces their ability to take charge of challenges. Providing assistance as needed and emphasizing their role in problem-solving builds self-reliance.

Reflecting on the Outcome:

Encouraging children to reflect on the results of their chosen solution promotes learning and growth. By discussing what worked well, what could be improved, and what they learned from the experience, children develop a deeper understanding of problem-solving.

Encouraging Perseverance:

Instilling a sense of perseverance is crucial in teaching problem-solving skills. Emphasizing that not all problems have immediate solutions and encouraging children to persist in the face of challenges nurtures resilience and determination.

Modelling Problem-Solving:

Children learn by observing the behaviour of significant adults in their lives. Modelling effective problem-solving by openly discussing challenges and demonstrating how to approach them teaches children valuable problem-solving strategies.

This approach not only equips children with valuable life skills but also promotes independence, resilience, and a positive attitude towards challenges. Teaching problem-solving skills lays the groundwork for success in various aspects of life and empowers children to thrive in an ever-changing world.

Practical Activities to Foster Problem-Solving Skills in Children:

Fostering problem-solving skills in children is essential for their cognitive development and overall growth. Engaging them in practical activities that require critical thinking, creativity, and strategic decision-making can significantly enhance their problem-solving abilities. Here's an in-depth exploration of practical activities designed to foster problem-solving skills in children:

Scenario Role-Playing:

Creating scenarios where children act out real-life problems allows them to brainstorm and implement solutions, promoting critical thinking and decision-making skills. This hands-on approach enables children to apply problem-solving strategies in a fun and interactive way.

Problem-Solving Board Game:

Playing board games that involve strategic decision-making provides a playful environment for reinforcing problem-solving skills. Games like chess or strategic board games require children to analyse situations, anticipate outcomes, and make informed choices, enhancing their problem-solving abilities.

Family Decision-Making:

Involving children in family decisions, such as planning meals or outings, encourages active participation and critical thinking. Discussing potential solutions together allows children to contribute their ideas and perspectives, fostering collaboration and problem-solving skills.

Puzzle Challenges:

Providing age-appropriate puzzles that require problem-solving enhances spatial reasoning and cognitive skills. Puzzles require children to analyse patterns, manipulate objects, and think critically to find solutions, strengthening their problem-solving abilities.

DIY Projects:

Engaging in do-it-yourself (DIY) projects encourages children to figure out steps and overcome challenges, fostering creative problem-solving. Whether building a birdhouse or creating artwork, DIY projects provide opportunities for hands-on problem-solving experiences.

Collaborative Art:

Creating collaborative artwork where children need to problem-solve together fosters teamwork and effective communication.

Collaborative art projects encourage children to share ideas, negotiate solutions, and work towards a common goal, promoting problem-solving skills in a social context.

Nature Exploration:

Taking nature walks and encouraging children to observe and solve challenges they encounter, such as finding a way over an obstacle or identifying plants, promotes problem-solving skills in real-world settings. Nature exploration allows children to apply problem-solving strategies while connecting with the environment.

Mystery Box:

Placing random objects in a box and asking children to come up with creative uses for each item sparks imaginative problem-solving. This activity encourages children to think outside the box, explore different possibilities, and develop innovative solutions to challenges.

Math Problem Puzzles:

Presenting math problems in a puzzle format combines numerical challenges with critical thinking, making problem-solving enjoyable. Math problem puzzles encourage children to apply mathematical concepts in practical situations, enhancing their problem-solving skills.

Scavenger Hunt:

Organizing scavenger hunts with clues that require problem-solving promotes teamwork and strategic thinking. Scavenger hunts provide opportunities for children to work collaboratively, analyse clues, and solve challenges, strengthening their problem-solving abilities.

Building Challenges:

Providing building blocks or construction materials and assigning challenges like building the tallest tower or a structure that can withstand weight encourages children to think critically and creatively. Building challenges allow children to experiment, problem-solve, and innovate, fostering their problem-solving skills in a hands-on manner.

Role Model Stories:

Sharing stories about historical figures or fictional characters who demonstrated effective problem-solving inspires creative thinking and critical analysis. Discussing these stories with children helps them understand problem-solving strategies and apply them to their own lives, promoting resilience and adaptability.

Invention Time:

Allocating time for children to invent or improve something encourages creativity and problem-solving skills. Whether designing a new invention or improving an existing one, invention time allows children to explore solutions to real-world problems and unleash their innovative potential.

Critical Thinking Games:

Introducing games that involve critical thinking, such as chess or strategic board games, enhances problem-solving skills in a fun and engaging way. Critical thinking games require children to analyse situations, strategize, and make decisions, strengthening their problem-solving abilities while enjoying interactive gameplay.

Technology-Based Challenges:

Using educational apps or online platforms that present challenges requiring logical thinking and problem-solving skills provides children with interactive learning experiences. Technology-based challenges engage children in problem-solving activities tailored to their interests and abilities, promoting skill development in a digital environment.

Daily Decision Journal:

Encouraging children to keep a decision journal where they record daily choices and solutions fosters self-reflection and awareness. Reflecting on past decisions helps children develop a deeper understanding of their problem-solving process and learn from their experiences, enhancing their decision-making skills over time.

Emotional Problem-Solving:

Discussing emotional situations and asking children how they would handle them promotes problem-solving skills in interpersonal relationships. Helping children navigate emotional challenges encourages empathy, communication, and conflict resolution skills, strengthening their ability to solve problems in social contexts.

Community Problem-Solving:

Engaging in community service or projects that require problem-solving teaches children the impact of their solutions on a larger scale. Community problem-solving activities allow children to apply their problem-solving skills to real-world issues, fostering a sense of social responsibility and civic engagement.

Maze Challenges:

Creating or finding mazes that children must navigate enhances spatial awareness and logical reasoning. Maze challenges require children to analyse patterns, make decisions, and adapt their strategies, promoting problem-solving skills in a dynamic and engaging way.

Story Creation:

Encouraging children to write or narrate stories where characters encounter and resolve problems stimulates imaginative problem-solving. Story creation allows children to explore different scenarios, develop creative solutions, and express their ideas, fostering problem-solving skills in a creative and expressive format.

These practical activities offer a diverse range of experiences for children to develop and apply problem-solving skills in various contexts. By engaging in these activities, children not only enhance their problem-solving abilities but also cultivate resilience, creativity, and a positive attitude towards challenges. Nurturing problem-solving skills equips children with essential tools for success in academics, relationships, and life, empowering them to overcome obstacles and thrive in an ever-changing world.

"Discipline is helping a child solve a problem.
Punishment is making a child suffer for having a
problem. To raise problem solvers, focus on solutions not
retribution… "

3.6 Implementing Consistent Discipline:

Implementing consistent discipline in kids is crucial for their overall development and well-being. Consistency provides structure, guidance, and boundaries that help children navigate the complexities of life, teaching them valuable lessons about responsibility, accountability, and self-control. Here's a detailed exploration of the importance of implementing consistent discipline:

- **Establishing Boundaries:** Consistent discipline helps children understand acceptable behaviour and sets clear boundaries. By consistently enforcing rules, parents and caregivers create a predictable environment where children know what is expected of them, fostering a sense of security and stability.

- **Promoting Responsibility:** When children face consistent consequences for their actions, they learn to take responsibility for their behaviour. Knowing that their actions have predictable outcomes encourages them to think before they act and consider the consequences of their choices.

- **Building Self-Discipline:** Consistent discipline teaches children self-discipline and self-control. As they learn to regulate their behaviour to avoid negative consequences, they develop important skills for managing impulses, delaying gratification, and making thoughtful decisions.

- **Encouraging Accountability:** By consistently enforcing rules and consequences, parents and caregivers teach children about accountability. Children learn that their actions have repercussions, and they must take ownership of their behaviour, whether positive or negative.

- **Supporting Emotional Regulation:** Consistent discipline provides a framework for children to learn how to regulate their emotions effectively. When they understand the consequences of their actions and how to modify their behaviour accordingly, they develop resilience and coping strategies for handling challenging situations.

- **Fostering Respect:** Consistent discipline promotes mutual respect between children and authority figures. When rules are consistently enforced with fairness and empathy, children learn to respect the authority of their parents and caregivers while feeling respected and valued themselves.

- **Preparing for Adulthood:** Learning to follow rules and accept consequences is essential for success in adulthood. Consistent discipline helps children develop the skills and mind-set they need to thrive in school, work, and relationships, laying the foundation for responsible citizenship and productive participation in society.

- **Enhancing Family Dynamics:** Consistent discipline contributes to harmonious family dynamics by promoting cooperation, communication, and mutual understanding. When rules are consistently enforced, conflicts are minimized, and family members learn to trust and rely on each other.

Strategies to implement Consistent Discipline in kids:

Implementing consistent discipline is essential for nurturing responsible behaviour and accountability in children. It provides a structured framework for guiding their actions, teaching them the importance of rules, and helping them understand the consequences of their behaviour. Here's a comprehensive look at strategies to effectively implement consistent discipline:

1. Establish Clear Expectations:

Setting clear expectations and rules is the foundation of consistent discipline. Ensure that your child understands what behaviours are acceptable and what are not. Holding a family meeting to discuss and outline household rules in language appropriate to their age helps establish clarity.

2. Be Consistent:

Consistency is paramount in effective discipline. Enforce rules consistently so that children understand that the consequences for specific behaviours remain the same. If a rule is broken, consistently apply the predetermined consequence to help children connect actions with outcomes.

3. Positive Reinforcement:

Acknowledging and rewarding positive behaviour reinforces responsible conduct. Praise your child when they follow the rules or exhibit positive behaviour, using specific and encouraging language to highlight their efforts.

4. Natural Consequences:

Allowing children to experience the natural consequences of their actions teaches responsibility and accountability. For example, if a child forgets their lunch, allowing them to experience hunger helps them learn the importance of being prepared.

5. Logical Consequences:

Implementing logical consequences directly related to the misbehaviour helps children understand the connection between actions and outcomes. For instance, if a child refuses to clean up toys, a logical consequence may be temporarily limiting access to those toys.

6. Time-Outs:

Time-outs provide children with a brief break to reflect on their behaviour, helping them calm down and consider the consequences of their actions. Designate a specific area for time-outs and keep the duration age-appropriate and consistent.

7. Loss of Privileges:

Connect misbehaviour with the loss of privileges to reinforce the idea that privileges are earned through responsible behaviour. For example, if a child does not complete their homework, they may lose screen time or other privileges until the task is finished.

8. Communicate Effectively:

Maintain open and clear communication with your child about rules and consequences, fostering understanding. Discuss the reasons behind rules calmly; ensuring your child understands the expectations and the rationale behind them.

9. Be Firm but Loving:

Discipline should be delivered with firmness but accompanied by love and understanding. Children should feel supported even when facing consequences. Maintain a calm tone while enforcing rules and express your love, reassuring the child that discipline is meant to help them learn and grow.

By incorporating these strategies into your parenting approach, you create a supportive environment for consistent and effective discipline. Remember that discipline is a tool for teaching, guiding, and nurturing children, and it is most impactful when delivered with love, understanding, and a focus on the child's overall development.

Practical Activities to Reinforce Consistent Discipline:

- **Behaviour Chart:**

    o   Activity: Create a visual behaviour chart with clear expectations and rewards. Children can earn stickers or points for positive behaviour, fostering a sense of accomplishment.

- **Family Meetings:**

    o   Activity: Hold regular family meetings to discuss and collaboratively set rules. Encourage open communication, allowing children to express their thoughts on rules and consequences.

- **Positive Note Jar:**

    o   Activity: Establish a "Positive Note Jar" where family members can write uplifting notes about each other. Read these notes together regularly, reinforcing positive behaviour.

- **Responsibility Board:**

    o   Activity: Designate a responsibility board with age-appropriate tasks. Children can choose tasks and earn privileges upon completion, teaching them about accountability.

- **Role Play:**

    o   Activity: Engage in role-playing scenarios where children act out positive and negative behaviours. This interactive approach helps them understand consequences and alternatives.

- **Consequence Discussion:**

  - Activity: After misbehaviour, have a calm discussion with the child about the consequences. Ask questions like, "What happened?" and "What could have been done differently?"

- **Family Contract:**

  - Activity: Create a family contract outlining rules, consequences, and rewards. Involve children in drafting the contract, promoting a sense of ownership and responsibility.

- **Goal Setting:**

  - Activity: Set achievable behaviour goals with children. Discuss the steps needed to reach these goals and celebrate successes together, reinforcing positive behaviour.

- **Problem-Solving Games:**

  - Activity: Introduce problem-solving games that require collaboration and decision-making. This helps children develop critical thinking skills and understand consequences.

- **Role Model Discussions:**

  - Activity: Choose a positive role model or character and discuss their traits with children. Encourage them to emulate these qualities in their own behaviour.

- **Family Appreciation Night:**

  o Activity: Designate a night where family members express appreciation for each other's positive behaviours. This encourages positive reinforcement within the family.

- **Journaling:**

  o Activity: Encourage children to keep a journal where they reflect on their behaviour and set personal goals for improvement. Review and discuss these journals regularly.

- **Shared Responsibilities:**

  o Activity: Involve children in daily responsibilities such as meal preparation or household chores. This instils a sense of responsibility and accountability.

- **Behaviour Reflection Sheets:**

  o Activity: Provide behaviour reflection sheets after misbehaviour. Ask children to write or draw their thoughts on the incident, fostering self-awareness.

- **Family Awards Ceremony:**

  o Activity: Organize a family awards ceremony where everyone is recognized for their positive contributions. This creates a positive atmosphere and reinforces good behaviour.

- **Storytelling:**

  - Activity: Share stories or fables with moral lessons. Discuss the consequences of characters' actions, prompting children to reflect on their own behaviour.

- **Personal Responsibility Pledge:**

  - Activity: Create a personal responsibility pledge that children can recite daily. This reinforces the importance of accountability and positive behaviour.

- **Mindfulness Practices:**

  - Activity: Introduce mindfulness practices such as deep breathing or meditation. These activities help children regulate their emotions and make thoughtful decisions.

- **Collaborative Rule Art:**

  - Activity: Create collaborative artwork featuring family rules. Display this artwork prominently, serving as a visual reminder of behavioural expectations.

- **Gratitude Circle:**

  - Activity: Form a gratitude circle where each family member expresses gratitude for another. This fosters positivity and strengthens family bonds.

These practical activities complement the strategies for consistent discipline, making the learning experience enjoyable for children while reinforcing the principles of responsible behaviour.

"Consistency is the key to Success…"

"Discipline is the bridge between goals and accomplishment…"

3.7 Fostering Independence in Children:

Fostering independence in children is not just about promoting autonomy; it's about equipping them with essential life skills that pave the way for success and resilience. Independence empowers children to navigate life's challenges confidently, make responsible decisions, and adapt to changing circumstances. Here's an in-depth exploration of the importance of fostering independence and effective strategies to achieve it:

- **Cultivating Self-Reliance:** Independence cultivates self-reliance by empowering children to take charge of their actions and decisions. When children learn to rely on themselves, they develop a sense of confidence and competence that serves them well in various aspects of life.

- **Instilling Responsibility:** Through independence, children learn to be accountable for their choices and actions. By giving them opportunities to make decisions and face consequences, parents teach children the importance of taking responsibility for their behaviour, fostering a sense of accountability from an early age.

- **Nurturing Resilience:** Independence plays a crucial role in building resilience. When children learn to solve problems, overcome obstacles, and bounce back from setbacks independently, they develop the resilience needed to thrive in the face of adversity and uncertainty.

- **Enhancing Critical Thinking:** Independence encourages critical thinking skills as children learn to assess situations, weigh options, and make informed decisions on their own. By fostering independent thinking, parents empower children to become confident and resourceful problem-solvers.

- **Boosting Confidence:** Successfully navigating challenges and making independent decisions builds children's confidence in their abilities. This self-assurance becomes a driving force that empowers them to take on new opportunities, pursue their goals, and face challenges with resilience and optimism.

- **Preparing for Adulthood:** Independence prepares children for the responsibilities and demands of adulthood. By equipping them with essential life skills, such as decision-making, time management, and problem-solving, parents ensure that children are well-prepared to navigate the complexities of adult life with confidence and competence.

Strategies to Foster Independence in children:

To foster independence in children, parents can implement a variety of strategies tailored to their child's age, abilities, and developmental stage:

- **Encouraging Decision-Making:** Provide children with opportunities to make age-appropriate decisions, such as choosing their clothes or selecting activities. Encourage them to weigh options, consider consequences, and take ownership of their choices.
- **Assigning Age-Appropriate Tasks:** Give children responsibilities around the house, such as setting the table, doing laundry, or tidying their room. These tasks not only teach children valuable life skills but also instill a sense of contribution and responsibility.
- **Teaching Problem-Solving:** Help children develop problem-solving skills by encouraging them to identify problems, brainstorm solutions, and evaluate outcomes. Offer guidance and support as needed, but allow children to take the lead in finding solutions to challenges they encounter.
- **Promoting Self-Help Skills:** Teach children basic self-care tasks, such as dressing themselves, brushing their teeth, and packing their school bag. Gradually increase their independence by encouraging them to handle these tasks without constant supervision.

- **Supporting Learning from Mistakes:** Create a supportive environment where mistakes are viewed as opportunities for learning and growth. Encourage children to reflect on their experiences, identify lessons learned, and apply them to future situations.

- **Establishing Routines:** Establish daily routines that provide structure and predictability for children. Routines help children learn to manage their time and responsibilities independently, fostering a sense of autonomy and self-discipline.

- **Encouraging Goal-Setting:** Support children in setting and pursuing goals that are meaningful to them. Help them develop action plans, track their progress, and celebrate their achievements, reinforcing the connection between effort and success.

- **Providing Financial Responsibility:** Introduce children to basic financial concepts and give them opportunities to manage money, such as saving allowance or making small purchases. Teach them the value of budgeting, saving, and making thoughtful spending decisions.

- **Promoting Open Communication:** Create an open and supportive environment where children feel comfortable expressing their thoughts, feelings, and concerns. Listen actively, validate their experiences, and offer guidance and encouragement as needed.

- **Modelling Independence:** Lead by example by demonstrating responsible decision-making, effective problem-solving, and self-care practices. Show children that independence is a valuable and achievable goal by modelling independent behaviours in your own life.

Fostering independence in children is a multifaceted process that requires patience, guidance, and support from parents and caregivers. By recognizing the importance of independence and implementing effective strategies to nurture it, parents empower children to become confident, responsible, and resilient individuals who are equipped to thrive in an ever-changing world.

Activities to promote Independence in children:

Certainly, fostering independence in kids involves engaging them in activities that gradually encourage self-reliance and decision-making. Here are some activities to promote independence in children:

- **Create a Morning Routine:**

  - *Activity:* Develop a morning routine chart with tasks like getting dressed, brushing teeth, and making the bed.
  - *Objective:* Encourages children to take charge of their morning responsibilities independently.

- **Cook Together:**

  - *Activity:* Involve children in simple cooking tasks like preparing sandwiches or mixing ingredients.
  - *Objective:* Teaches basic kitchen skills and fosters a sense of accomplishment.

- **Choose Outfits for the Week:**

  - *Activity:* Allow children to pick out their outfits for the week and organize them in their wardrobe.

o   *Objective:* Promotes decision-making and planning ahead.

- **Set the Table:**

  o   *Activity:* Assign the task of setting the table before meals.

  o   *Objective:* Instills a sense of responsibility and contributes to family routines.

- **Plan a Family Outing:**

  o   *Activity:* Let children take the lead in planning a family outing or activity.

  o   *Objective:* Encourages decision-making, organization, and collaboration.

- **Manage a Pet's Care:**

  o   *Activity:* If you have a pet, involve children in tasks like feeding, grooming, and walking (if applicable).

  o   *Objective:* Teaches responsibility and empathy towards animals.

- **Create a Chore Chart:**

  o   *Activity:* Develop a chore chart with age-appropriate tasks for each family member.

  o   *Objective:* Fosters a sense of contribution and accountability.

- **Plant and Care for a Garden:**

  o   *Activity:* Allocate a small space for a garden and involve children in planting and caring for plants.

- o *Objective:* Teaches responsibility and provides a hands-on experience with nature.

- **Create a Weekly Schedule:**

  - o *Activity:* Work together to create a weekly schedule with designated times for homework, play, and chores.
  - o *Objective:* Introduces time management and planning skills.

- **Handle Money:**

  - o *Activity:* Give children a small allowance and help them budget for simple purchases.
  - o *Objective:* Introduces financial responsibility and basic math skills.

- **Navigate Public Transportation:**

  - o *Activity:* Teach older children how to use public transportation for short trips.
  - o *Objective:* Builds confidence and independence in navigating the community.

- **Plan a Snack or Lunch:**

  - o *Activity:* Allow children to plan and prepare a simple snack or lunch.
  - o *Objective:* Enhances kitchen skills and decision-making.

- **Self-Check Homework:**

  - o *Activity:* Encourage children to review and correct their homework before submitting it.

- *Objective:* Promotes responsibility and attention to detail.

- **Organize Personal Items:**

  - *Activity:* Teach children to organize their backpacks, toys, or personal belongings.
  - *Objective:* Cultivates organizational skills and a sense of ownership.

Remember, the key is to gradually introduce these activities, considering the child's age and abilities. These experiences contribute to building a foundation for independence and self-confidence.

"Children can ask a thousand questions that even the wisest man cannot answer..."

3.8 Nurturing Emotional Intelligence in Children:

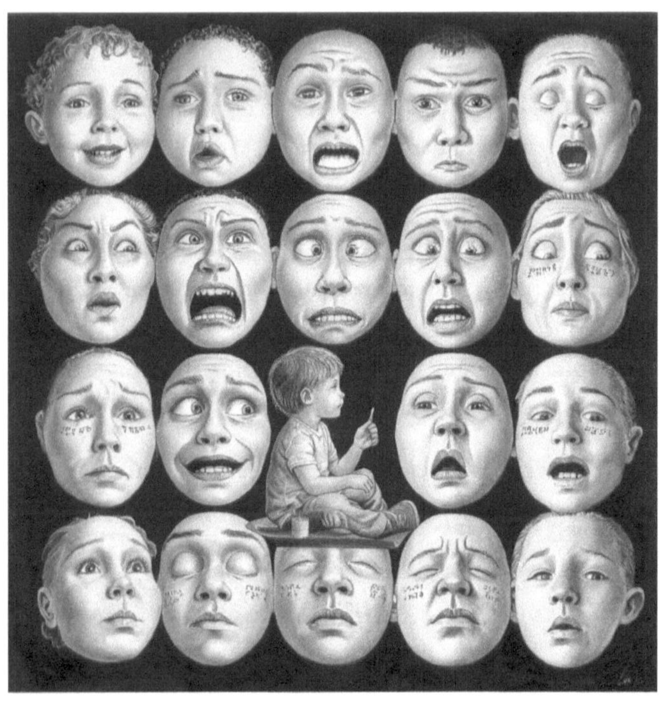

Emotional intelligence (EI) stands as a critical pillar of a child's holistic development, surpassing mere academic success. It encompasses a child's capacity to perceive, comprehend, and manage their own emotions, as well as their ability to empathize with others. Nurturing emotional intelligence in children is paramount as it lays the groundwork for healthy relationships, effective communication, and overall well-being.

The importance of fostering emotional intelligence in children cannot be overstated. Firstly, EI enhances self-awareness by enabling children to recognize and understand their emotions. This heightened self-awareness leads to improved self-regulation and a deeper understanding of personal strengths and weaknesses, empowering children to navigate social interactions and academic challenges more effectively.

Emotional intelligence allows children to empathize with others, fostering positive interpersonal relationships. By understanding and connecting with the emotions of those around them, children develop strengthened social bonds, increased cooperation, and a sense of community, all of which are crucial for their social and emotional development.

Effective communication is another key aspect influenced by emotional intelligence. By enabling children to express themselves and understand others' emotions, EI contributes to improved conflict resolution, enhanced teamwork, and the development of strong interpersonal skills. These skills form the foundation for healthy relationships and successful collaboration in various aspects of life.

Emotional intelligence equips children with the tools to navigate challenges, setbacks, and stressors more effectively, fostering resilience. By managing their emotions and coping with adversity in a healthy manner, children develop greater adaptability and a positive approach to overcoming obstacles, essential qualities for their personal growth and well-being.

Emotional intelligence also plays a crucial role in promoting mental health and emotional well-being. Children who possess strong EI are better equipped to manage stress, regulate their emotions, and maintain positive self-esteem, reducing the risk of mental health issues such as anxiety and depression.

Furthermore, Emotional intelligence enhances decision-making skills by encouraging children to consider both their own emotions and the consequences of their actions. This leads to improved decision-making, increased accountability, and a sense of personal responsibility, empowering children to make thoughtful and responsible choices in various aspects of their lives.

Strategies for Nurturing Emotional Intelligence in Children:

Nurturing Emotional intelligence (EI) in children is essential for their overall well-being and success in life. Here, we delve into various strategies that parents can employ to foster emotional intelligence effectively:

- **Model Emotional Awareness:** Parents and caregivers should openly express their own emotions and discuss how they manage them. Children learn by observing, and modelling emotional awareness sets a positive example for them to follow.

- **Teach Emotional Vocabulary:** Introduce a wide range of emotions and their corresponding words to expand children's emotional vocabulary. This enhances their ability to identify and articulate their feelings accurately.

- **Encourage Open Communication:** Create a safe and non-judgmental space for children to share their emotions freely. Open communication fosters trust and helps children feel understood and supported.

- **Practice Active Listening:** Teach and model active listening skills, emphasizing empathy and validation of children's emotions. Active listening promotes understanding and strengthens the parent-child bond.

- **Provide Tools for Self-Regulation:** Teach mindfulness techniques, deep breathing exercises, or journaling for self-regulation. These tools empower children to calm themselves and manage their emotions in challenging situations.

- **Use Literature and Media:** Explore books, movies, or shows that depict diverse emotional experiences. Stories provide a platform for discussing and understanding various emotions, promoting empathy and emotional literacy.

- **Celebrate Emotional Expression:** Reinforce the idea that all emotions are valid and should be expressed appropriately. Accepting a range of emotions promotes emotional authenticity and helps children develop a healthy relationship with their feelings.

- **Role-Playing Scenarios:** Engage in role-playing scenarios to practice recognizing and responding to emotions in real-life situations. Role-playing enhances emotional intelligence by applying knowledge in practical contexts.

- **Foster Empathy Through Service:** Engage in community service or volunteer work to cultivate empathy. Acts of service provide opportunities for children to understand and respond to others' emotions, fostering compassion and empathy.

- **Set Emotional Intelligence Goals:** Encourage children to set goals for developing specific emotional intelligence skills, such as identifying and managing their emotions or empathizing with others. Goal-setting promotes intentional growth and self-reflection.

- **Provide Positive Reinforcement**: Acknowledge and reinforce positive expressions of emotional intelligence, such as effectively managing emotions or showing empathy towards others. Positive reinforcement motivates children to continue developing their emotional skills.

- **Create a 'Feelings' Journal:** Have children keep a journal to record their emotions and reflections. Journaling promotes self-awareness, reflection, and emotional expression.

- **Establish Mindful Practices:** Introduce mindfulness exercises, such as guided meditation or body scans, to enhance emotional self-awareness and regulation. Mindfulness practices help children develop a greater sense of calm and resilience.

- **Encourage Perspective-Taking:** Prompt discussions about situations from different perspectives to help children understand and empathize with others' emotions. Perspective-taking builds empathy and promotes social understanding.

- **Support Emotional Growth in Play:** Utilize play as a context for exploring and expressing emotions. Play allows children to experiment with different emotional scenarios in a safe and supportive environment, promoting emotional intelligence and creativity.

- **Seek Professional Guidance if Needed:** If concerns arise about a child's emotional development, seek guidance from mental health professionals. Professional support can provide additional strategies and interventions to support emotional growth and well-being.

By incorporating these strategies into daily interactions and activities, parents, caregivers, and educators can effectively nurture emotional intelligence in children, equipping them with essential skills for lifelong success and well-being.

"Emotional regulation is not a skill set that we are born with… But with connection, it is never too late to learn…"

"For children to have success; it's more than just Academics… It takes Social-Emotional Intelligence…"

3.9 Understanding and Cultivating Empathy in Children:

Empathy, often described as the ability to understand and share the feelings of others, is a crucial trait that lays the foundation for the development of emotionally intelligent and socially adept individuals. It goes beyond mere sympathy or pity; empathy involves truly comprehending another person's emotions and experiences, thereby forming a deep connection with them. Instilling empathy in children is not merely a desirable quality but a fundamental life skill that profoundly shapes their relationships, communication abilities, and overall worldview. Effective parenting involves recognizing the importance of empathy and implementing strategies that foster its growth in children, thereby contributing to their holistic development.

Importance of Nurturing Empathy in Children:

The significance of empathy in the growth of children spans across various domains, each of which plays a vital role in their overall well-being and success:

- **Building Meaningful Relationships:** Empathy serves as the bedrock of meaningful relationships. Children who possess empathetic abilities can understand and resonate with the feelings of others, thus fostering deeper connections with peers, family members, and the broader community. By empathizing with others, children develop a sense of trust, compassion, and camaraderie, which are essential for building strong and lasting relationships.

- **Effective Communication:** Empathy enhances communication skills by enabling children to not only express themselves effectively but also understand the perspectives and emotions of others. When children can empathize with others, they become better equipped to communicate their thoughts, feelings, and needs in a manner that is respectful and empathetic. This fosters healthy interpersonal dynamics characterized by mutual understanding and respect.

- **Conflict Resolution:** An empathetic mind-set plays a crucial role in conflict resolution. Children who possess empathy can perceive and validate the emotions of others involved in a conflict, which allows them to approach the situation with compassion and understanding. By considering the perspectives and feelings of all parties involved, empathetic children are more likely to find constructive solutions to conflicts, thereby creating harmonious environments and fostering positive relationships.

- **Promoting Compassion:** Empathy nurtures compassion in children, leading them to show kindness, offer support, and actively contribute to creating a compassionate and inclusive community. When children can empathize with others, they are more inclined to engage in pro-social behaviours and demonstrate acts of kindness and altruism. This not only benefits the individuals receiving compassion but also contributes to the overall well-being of society as a whole.

- **Cultivating Emotional Intelligence:** Empathy is a fundamental component of emotional intelligence, which encompasses the ability to recognize, understand, and manage one's own emotions as well as those of others. Children who develop empathy demonstrate a heightened emotional awareness, enabling them to navigate and regulate their emotions effectively. By empathizing with others, children learn to recognize and validate a wide range of emotions, which is essential for developing resilience, empathy, and overall emotional well-being.

Empathy plays a pivotal role in the growth and development of children, shaping their relationships, communication skills, conflict resolution abilities, compassion, and emotional intelligence. By recognizing the significance of empathy and implementing strategies to foster its growth in children, parents and caregivers can empower them to become empathetic, compassionate, and emotionally intelligent individuals capable of thriving in today's interconnected world.

Strategies to Nurture Empathy in Children:

Fostering empathy in children is crucial for their social and emotional development. Here are some practical strategies to help cultivate empathy in your child as part of your parenting journey:

1. **Model Empathetic Behaviour:** Children learn by example, so demonstrate empathy in your interactions with others. Show kindness, understanding, and compassion in your own actions and conversations.
2. **Encourage Perspective-Taking:** Help your child understand different points of view by asking questions like, "How do you think they feel?" or "Why do you

think they acted that way?" This encourages empathy by promoting the ability to see things from another person's perspective.

3. **Teach Emotional Literacy:** Help your child identify and express their own emotions, as well as recognize the emotions of others. Use emotional vocabulary to label feelings and discuss how different emotions can influence behaviour.

4. **Practice Active Listening:** Encourage your child to listen attentively when others are speaking and to show that they understand by paraphrasing or summarizing what was said. This demonstrates respect and validation for others' experiences and emotions.

5. **Promote Kindness and Generosity:** Encourage acts of kindness and generosity towards others, whether it's sharing toys, helping a friend in need, or performing random acts of kindness in the community. Highlight the positive impact these actions have on others.

6. **Expose Them to Diverse Perspectives:** Introduce your child to diverse cultures, backgrounds, and experiences through books, movies, and real-life interactions. This helps broaden their understanding of the world and fosters empathy towards people who are different from them.

7. **Encourage Problem-Solving Skills:** Teach your child to resolve conflicts peacefully and considerately. Help them brainstorm solutions that take into account the needs and feelings of all parties involved.

8. **Set Clear Boundaries:** Establish clear expectations for behaviour and consequences for actions that hurt others. Consistently reinforce empathy as a value

in your family and address any instances of unkind behaviour promptly.

9. **Encourage Empathetic Play:** Provide opportunities for your child to engage in role-playing or imaginative play where they can pretend to be someone else and experience different perspectives and emotions.

10. **Acknowledge and Praise Empathetic Behaviour:** Notice and praise instances when your child demonstrates empathy towards others. Positive reinforcement reinforces the value of empathy and encourages its continued development.

By incorporating these strategies into your parenting approach, you can help nurture your child's capacity for empathy and compassion, laying the foundation for positive relationships and emotional intelligence throughout their lives.

"Empathy has no script... No right way or wrong way...
It's simply listening, holding space without Judgement,
emotionally connecting, and communicating that
incredibly healing message of 'you are not alone...' "

Chapter 4

Cultivating Strong Bonds and Holistic Development

4.1   The Importance of Quality Time with Kids:

Quality time with kids holds immense importance in parenting, as it goes beyond the sheer quantity of time spent together, emphasizing the significance of meaningful, focused interactions. While the amount of time invested in parenting is essential, the nature and quality of that time play an equally crucial role in nurturing strong emotional bonds, contributing to holistic development, and leaving a lasting impact on a child's growth and well-being.

One of the primary reasons why quality time matters is its role in strengthening the emotional connection between parents and children. By engaging in purposeful interactions, parents create a secure emotional bond that promotes a sense of safety and trust, which are essential for healthy development. Positive reinforcement of desired behaviours during focused interactions acknowledges and values children, reinforcing positive patterns of behaviour and contributing to their emotional growth.

Quality time contributes to holistic development by addressing various aspects of a child's well-being, including emotional, intellectual, and social needs. Meaningful conversations and shared activities during quality time enhance children's communication skills, enabling them to express themselves effectively and understand others. Positive experiences created during quality time also form the foundation of a child's worldview, contributing to emotional resilience and a positive outlook on life.

Regular, focused interactions build a foundation of trust between parents and children, which is fundamental for healthy relationships and emotional well-being. By implementing strategies for quality time, parents can create enriching moments that foster strong bonds and holistic development in their children.

These strategies include establishing rituals, practicing active listening, unplugging from technology, planning special activities, prioritizing family dinners, engaging in quality conversations, supporting hobbies, creating a safe space for communication, celebrating achievements, practicing mindful presence, implementing quality bedtime routines, conducting weekly family meetings, organizing educational outings, expressing affection regularly, and teaching life skills through daily activities.

The essence of quality time lies in the intention and focus devoted to shared moments. By prioritizing meaningful interactions and implementing effective strategies for quality time, parents lay the groundwork for their child's emotional resilience, intellectual growth, and overall well-being. It's not just about the minutes spent together but the lasting impact those moments have on a child's development.

"To be in your child's memories tomorrow, you have to be in their lives today…"

"Children don't need Perfection, they need Connection…"

4.2   Positive Role Modelling for Kids:

Positive role modelling is an essential aspect of shaping the character and values of children, as they are keen observers who often learn more from what they see in action than from what they hear. The significance of positive role modelling lies in its profound impact on various aspects of children's development, including behavioural learning, values and morality, emotional regulation, inspiration and aspiration, social skills, work ethic and success, among others.

Positive role models set behavioural standards for children by exemplifying desirable actions and attitudes. Children tend to imitate the behaviours of those they look up to, whether it's a parent, teacher, or another influential figure, thereby shaping their own conduct accordingly. Through observation, children learn the importance of honesty, kindness, empathy, and other virtues that contribute to their ethical development.

Positive role models exhibit emotional regulation, providing children with examples of how to manage their emotions effectively. By witnessing how their role models handle stress, frustration, and other emotional challenges, children learn valuable coping mechanisms and emotional resilience. Additionally, positive role models inspire and provide a source of aspiration for children. When children see someone they admire achieving goals or demonstrating perseverance, it instills a sense of motivation and belief in their own capabilities.

Positive role models often excel in interpersonal relationships, teaching children valuable social skills, effective communication, and conflict resolution strategies. Observing the work ethic and success of positive role models instills the importance of hard work, dedication, and continuous learning in children, fostering a sense of ambition and determination.

In reflection of positive role modelling in children, various patterns emerge. Children tend to mimic the behaviour of their role models, replicating actions, gestures, and language patterns they observe. Moreover, the values demonstrated by positive role models become internalized by children, guiding their decision-making and moral compass. Witnessing healthy emotional expressions and coping mechanisms contributes to children's emotional well-being, while positive role models also influence academic and personal growth.

To effectively implement positive role modelling, parents and caregivers can employ specific strategies. Consistency in actions is crucial, as positive role models must exhibit desirable behaviour consistently to reinforce its importance to children. Open communication, active listening, and the demonstration of values through actions are also vital components. Additionally, acknowledging and learning from mistakes, encouraging curiosity, setting achievable goals, displaying empathy and compassion, embracing inclusion and diversity, and demonstrating a healthy work-life balance are essential strategies for positive role modelling.

In the core, Positive role modelling is a dynamic and continuous process that significantly influences a child's development. By embodying desirable values, behaviours, and attitudes, positive role models contribute to the holistic growth of children, nurturing their character and shaping the individuals they become.

"The most powerful way to change the world is to live in front of your children the way we would like the world to be..."

"Many believe parenting is about controlling children's behaviour and training them to act like adults. But parenting is about controlling our own behaviour and acting like an adult ourselves. Children learn what they live and live what they learn..."

"Children don't listen to instruction of hypocrites; it is your actions that guide their actions, it is not your lectures or punishments... "

4.3 Self-Care for Parents: Nurturing the Caregivers for a Healthier Family Dynamic:

Self-care for parents is not merely a luxury but a fundamental necessity that plays a critical role in fostering a healthy family dynamic. In the whirlwind of parental responsibilities, it's easy for caregivers to prioritize their children's needs over their own well-being. However, practicing self-care isn't selfish; it's a strategic investment in the overall health and harmony of the family unit. Let's delve into the profound importance of self-care for parents and how it positively influences children.

The Importance of Self-Care for Parents:

1. **Emotional Resilience:** Regular self-care activities help parents manage stress and enhance emotional resilience. By modelling effective coping mechanisms, parents teach children valuable skills for navigating life's challenges.

2. **Physical Health:** Prioritizing physical well-being through exercise, nutrition, and rest ensures that parents can actively engage in family activities, promoting a positive and active lifestyle for children.

3. **Mental Well-Being:** Taking time for mental relaxation and leisure pursuits alleviates parental burnout and promotes mental health, providing a stable and nurturing environment for children.

4. **Setting Boundaries:** Establishing boundaries and recognizing personal needs create a healthy balance between caregiving and self-care. Children learn the importance of setting limits and respecting individual needs, fostering a sense of autonomy.

5. **Improved Patience:** Regular self-care practices enhance patience and emotional regulation. Patient parents model effective communication and conflict resolution, positively influencing children's behaviour.

6. **Enhanced Productivity:** Taking breaks and recharging boosts cognitive function and productivity. Focused parents can better assist with homework, engage in enriching activities, and contribute to their children's academic growth.

7. **Positive Role Modelling:** Prioritizing self-care sets a positive example for children, emphasizing the importance of individual well-being. Children are

more likely to adopt healthy habits and self-care practices as they observe their parents prioritizing personal wellness.

8. **Cultivating Joy:** Engaging in activities that bring joy and fulfilment enhances overall life satisfaction. Joyful parents contribute to a positive home atmosphere, creating a nurturing environment for children to thrive.

Reflections on Children:

1. **Emotional Intelligence:** Children exposed to parents who practice self-care are likely to develop emotional intelligence, recognizing and managing their own emotions effectively.

2. **Healthy Coping Mechanisms:** Observing parents engage in self-care teaches children the importance of adopting healthy coping mechanisms when facing challenges.

3. **Balanced Lifestyle:** Children raised in an environment where self-care is valued are more likely to adopt a balanced and health-conscious lifestyle.

4. **Respect for Boundaries:** Parents who set boundaries and prioritize self-care teach children the significance of respecting others' limits.

5. **Communication Skills:** Children raised by parents who prioritize mental well-being are more likely to develop strong communication skills and interpersonal relationships.

6. **Positive Self-Image:** A parent's positive self-image, cultivated through self-care practices, contributes to a positive and empowering family culture.

7. **Stress Management:** Children learn effective stress management by witnessing parents engage in activities that promote relaxation and rejuvenation.

8. **Empathy and Compassion:** Parents who practice self-compassion through self-care activities model empathy, teaching children the importance of caring for oneself and others.

Strategies for Effective Self-Care:

- Establish a Routine: Schedule regular self-care activities into daily or weekly routines.
- Prioritize Sleep: Ensure adequate and quality sleep for physical and mental well-being.
- Delegate Responsibilities: Share caregiving responsibilities with a partner or seek support from friends and family.
- Mindful Practices: Incorporate mindfulness techniques into daily life for relaxation.
- Set Realistic Goals: Establish achievable personal and professional goals to avoid overwhelming stress.
- Seek Professional Support: Consult mental health professionals for guidance and support when needed.
- Connect with Others: Foster social connections through spending time with loved ones or participating in group activities.
- Engage in Hobbies: Dedicate time to activities that bring joy and fulfilment.
- Exercise Regularly: Prioritize physical activity for physical and mental health.
- Learn to Say No: Set boundaries by learning to decline additional commitments when necessary.

- Technology Detox: Take breaks from electronic devices to reduce stress.
- Self-Reflection: Engage in regular self-reflection to assess personal needs and goals.

Self-care for parents is indispensable for creating a harmonious and nurturing family environment. By prioritizing their own well-being, parents not only enhance their own lives but also impart invaluable lessons to their children. A family rooted in self-care cultivates emotional intelligence, resilience, and a holistic approach to well-being that resonates across generations.

"Being a parent is the best reason you will have to take care of yourself"

Here are some practical activities that parents and kids can engage in to enhance their parenting journey:

- **Family Meal Preparation**: Involve children in meal preparation activities such as grocery shopping, meal planning, and cooking. This not only teaches them valuable life skills but also provides an opportunity for quality family time.

- **Nature Walks:** Take regular walks or hikes in nature with your children. Use this time to explore the outdoors, observe wildlife, and engage in conversations about the environment and conservation.

- **Art and Craft Sessions:** Set aside time for creative activities such as drawing, painting, or crafting. Encourage children to express themselves artistically and showcase their creativity.

- **Reading Together:** Establish a routine of reading together as a family. Choose age-appropriate books and take turns reading aloud. Discuss the storylines, characters, and themes to promote literacy and critical thinking skills.

- **Family Game Nights:** Dedicate a night each week to playing board games or card games as a family. This promotes bonding, teamwork, and friendly competition while having fun together.

- **Volunteer Work:** Get involved in community service or volunteer projects as a family. This instills a sense of empathy, compassion, and social responsibility in children while making a positive impact on others.

- **Outdoor Adventures:** Plan outdoor adventures such as picnics, bike rides, or visits to local parks. Encourage exploration, physical activity, and appreciation for the natural world.

- **Journaling:** Start a family journal where everyone can write or draw about their thoughts, experiences, and memories. Reflect on past events and set goals for the future together.
- **Science Experiments:** Conduct simple science experiments at home to spark curiosity and excitement about the world around us. Explore topics such as gravity, chemistry, or plant growth through hands-on activities.
- **Music and Dance:** Have dance parties or music sessions where everyone can groove to their favourite tunes. Encourage children to explore different genres of music and express themselves through movement.
- **Mindfulness Exercises:** Practice mindfulness exercises together, such as deep breathing, meditation, or yoga. Use these techniques to promote relaxation, stress relief, and emotional well-being for both parents and children.
- **Family Meetings:** Hold regular family meetings to discuss important topics, make decisions together, and express thoughts and feelings in a safe and supportive environment.
- **Financial Planning:** Involve children in age-appropriate financial planning activities such as budgeting, saving, and setting financial goals. Teach them the value of money and responsible spending habits.
- **Cooking Lessons:** Teach children basic cooking skills by involving them in meal preparation. Start with simple recipes and gradually increase the complexity as they gain confidence in the kitchen.

- **Random Acts of Kindness:** Encourage random acts of kindness towards family members, friends, and strangers. Lead by example and demonstrate the importance of empathy, generosity, and compassion in everyday life.

By incorporating these practical activities into your parenting journey, you can strengthen family bonds, promote learning and growth, and create lasting memories with your children.

Conclusion

As we conclude this insightful exploration into the realm of efficient parenting, it is with the profound understanding that the journey of raising resilient, empathetic, and responsible individuals is both an art and a science. Through the pages of this guide, we've delved into the intricate web of modern parenting, threading our way through the challenges and triumphs that define the landscape of contemporary family life.

Efficient parenting, as elucidated in these pages, is not about perfection but about a purposeful and mindful approach. It is a journey marked by intentional choices, fostering an environment where children not only thrive but also contribute positively to the world around them. From navigating the digital dilemma to overcoming societal pressures, we've dissected the multifaceted challenges faced by parents in today's fast-paced world. This guide stands as a testament to the belief that parenting is not a one-size-fits-all endeavour, but a dynamic process that requires adaptability, understanding, and continuous learning.

The strategies presented here are not rigid directives but flexible tools, empowering parents to tailor their approach based on the unique needs and personalities of their children. We've journeyed through the importance of effective communication, setting clear boundaries, and fostering an environment of open-mindedness. Each insight and recommendation is designed to equip parents with practical, actionable steps – a toolkit for transformation in their personal parenting endeavours.

Our exploration touched upon the critical aspects of instilling resilience, emotional well-being, and a sense of responsibility in children. In a world saturated with screens and societal expectations, we've provided strategies for parents to not only survive but thrive in the demanding role of a modern-day parent.

As we bid farewell to this journey, remember that parenting is a dynamic adventure, filled with unexpected twists and turns. The key lies not in avoiding challenges but in navigating them with grace, wisdom, and a steadfast commitment to the well-being of our children. May this guide serve as a compass, guiding you through the uncharted waters of parenting, and may your journey be marked by moments of joy, growth, and the enduring bond that comes from raising good humans.

"Children are our greatest teachers. From them, we can learn some of life's most valuable qualities; patience, curiosity, kindness, determination, resilience, fearlessness, trust. And most importantly, they teach us what it means to love and to be loved…"

"Shine Bright: Illuminate Our Path with Your Reviews"

Dear Esteemed Reader,

As you delve into the heart-warming pages of "Raising Resilient Hearts," we embark on a journey together—one that celebrates the art of efficient parenting and the profound impact it has on shaping resilient, compassionate individuals. Your presence in this journey is invaluable, and we are deeply honoured to have you along our side. Your thoughts, experiences, and insights serve as guiding lights, illuminating our path and enriching our understanding of what it means to nurture resilient, empathetic souls. Your reviews are not just words on a page—they are beacons of inspiration, guiding fellow parents toward greater understanding, connection, and growth.

So, dear reader, we humbly invite you to share your thoughts and reflections on "Raising Resilient Hearts." Your reviews hold the power to ignite positive change, spark meaningful conversations, and foster a community of support and encouragement. Together, let us shine bright and illuminate the path forward, creating a world where every child is empowered to thrive and flourish.

Thank you for being an integral part of our journey. Your voice matters and your reviews have the power to make a difference.

Kindly pen down your reviews to, happyreads10@gmail.com

With heartfelt gratitude,

Niraimathi Magilmaran.